HOW TO BE A DICK

BY

CHRIS HARPER-MERCER

FORWARD BY

"SKUNK"

Copyright © 2016 by CHRIS HARPER-MERCER

All rights reserved.

ISBN **1537033484**
ISBN-13: 9781537033488

In this book, I may refer to a technique for getting rich or getting laid, without giving credit to the original asshole who came up with the idea. This is because I don't really give a fuck about who thought something up first. Copyrights? Suck my big green veiny donkey balls. Long live internet pirates, and getting unlimited free shit online.

Can you imagine if some guy was allowed to patent fire? And every time you sparked up a joint, this lame fucking dipshit demanded royalties? Fuck that noise. Information should be FREE!

FORWARD

My name is Frank, but my friends call me Skunk, because I always smell like marijuana.

I grow weed in my home, and grow even more weed in the outdoor wilderness that surrounds my hometown of Roseburg, Oregon. I sell weed to pay the bills.

I remember the first day I met Chris Harper-Mercer. It was July, 2014. I was in line at the Starbucks, on Garden Valley boulevard, across the street from the Fred Meyer store. Chris stood in line behind me, got a whiff of me, and said, "You smell good!"

I smiled, and introduced myself as Skunk. He seemed cool, and I was always looking for new customers to sell weed to. So I said, "Why don't we take our coffee to go, we could puff a joint in a secluded spot I know not far from here?"

I instantly liked Chris. He told the funniest stories. He had some very crazy opinions, but not once did I ever feel like he was dangerous. We would meet about once a month, and he would buy anywhere from a ½ ounce to a full ounce of weed from me. I have a policy, I don't sell to anyone that's "too busy" to smoke some with me.

I considered Chris to be my friend. We were both atheists, and we both thought all religionists were retarded.

We both didn't like blacks. Chris grew up in Los Angeles, where the black thugs would give him grief in school, beating on him, taking his bike and shit, you know, typical nigger bully shit.

I hated blacks because I got robbed by a nigger. This crackhead nigger pulls out a gun, so I give him all my money and weed. The punk motherfucker still pistol whipped me, giving me a bloody black eye and a chipped eye socket. For six months, the white part of my eye was full of blood. Every time I looked in the mirror, and saw my ruined face, I cursed all niggers. God how I hated them.

Anyway, Chris seemed like an ordinary guy to me. He just had some wild opinions, which made him kinda interesting to get high with. Or at least that's what I thought back then.

One day we were puffing weed on the banks of the Umpqua river. The river is popular for its beauty, and its crazy rapids that kayakers love. Chris tells me he wrote a book, and he's very excited. He explains that his book is about how to get rich and how to get laid.

I was surprised, because Chris was neither rich nor popular with girls.

He explained that it didn't matter if he was rich or not, as long as the readers BELIEVE he's rich.

Chris asked me to read his book, and give him my opinion. I said I would, and he gave me a thumbdrive, containing his manuscript, the manuscript you are holding now.

His book was strange. He claimed to be an old man in the book, and super rich. He claimed to have fucked a thousand women!

But perhaps the strangest thing about the book, is that he is constantly insulting the readers! He calls them every horrible name, and so I asked him why?

Chris just laughed, and said he was just being funny.

HOW TO BE A DICK

The last time I saw Chris was about 2 months before the shooting massacre. He totally became obsessed with this movie, "RAMPAGE", about a guy named Bill Williamson, who single-handedly kills an entire town. He was so animated, excited, he reminded me of someone I know who smokes meth.

He kinda creeped me out. Remember, I'm a super-laid-back pothead, and I'm way too stoned to think about killing anyone for real. That kind of talk ruins my deeply zen buzz!

So I admit I kinda blew him off after the Rampage talk. He'd call me or text me, and I'd claim to be busy, or I'd say that I'm out of weed temporarily.

Fast forward to October 2, 2015. I see the news story about the 9 people Chris killed. I'm freaking out big time. I fully expected the F.B.I. to ask me questions, but they never did. In my panic I threw away about 20 immature pot plants. :(

Now that all the dust has settled, and everyone knows he had no accomplices, I feel the world might benefit from reading this book. It is a peek into the mind of a mass murderer.

To the rest of the world, Chris will always be a Lone Wolf killer. But to me he was a friend, a troubled soul, and someone to be missed.

His book is presented before you now, unedited.

Sincerely,

Skunk

Skunk

Roseburg, Oregon

08/10/2016

1

How to Be a Better Dick

Nobody Likes a Dick

Let's face it. Being a Dick ain't easy. It's like we are the new niggers, we get treated like shit everywhere we go. Try to light up a cigarette in a diner, and suddenly everyone is on your ass about it. You go to work, and your boss' secretary found the toilet cam you hid in the ladies room. Then you try to pick up your date for the night, a cute little high school sophomore with big tits and ass, and her Dad is writing down your license plate number.

It's enough to make you feel like everyone is out to get you.

Haters gonna hate. They can miss me with that bullshit. But still, you might be starting to wonder if there's an easier way to get what you want. Maybe people around you are saying, "Hey, Dick, you are really pissing us off, please grow up and show a bit more restraint." Being a Dick is expensive, what with the court fines, alimony, lawsuits. And being a Dick can be downright painful, with the drunken beat-downs at the honky-tonk bar, the DUI accidents that messed up your neck and back, and the constant nagging from wives, girlfriends, neighbors, bosses, and parents.

But let us not lose sight of the prize! There is a good reason we are Dicks. We want to be rich. We want to screw lots of hot women. We want to retire with a mountain of cash, swimming in money like Scrooge McDuck. And everyone knows, there are two classes of people in the world- The Rich, and Everyone Else.

Donald Fuckin Trump, the King of the Dicks, didn't get to the top of Money Mountain by helping those in need. He didn't get there by playing nice, or compromising, or behaving in a reasonable, friendly manner. No. He got to the top by being a loudmouth, abusive, rude, arrogant, conceited, narcissistic orangutan asshole.

Yes, the path of the Dick is fraught with risk. Everyone is jealous of you. You have so many enemies, you lie awake at night wondering which crazy ex-girlfriend could have carved those nasty words into the paint of your corvette convertible. Guys at work get mad when you sprinkle rat droppings in their coffee, it's like they can't take a joke. And let's be honest, getting punched in the face on a regular basis, is enough to make you pause and reflect on your life decisions, and wonder if a better path to success exists.

I have good news! He is Risen!

Just kidding! Wouldn't that be funny, if this book was really a lame attempt at getting you to accept Jesus into your heart? No, I'm not that much of a Dick. But I do have some really good news. There is a better way. You can be a Dick, and get laid by badonkadonk bitches, and make mad money, without all the haters, the face-slaps, and the lawsuit hassles.

I am an Olde Dick. See how I spelled old? That's how old I am. I'm a wrinkly sack of venereal diseases and moldy smells. I'm a crustified, mummified, ancient Dick from Jurassic times. I'm older than your grandma's peppermint candy, the shit she keeps in the porcelain bowl on the coffee table, right next to the wax fruit.

HOW TO BE A DICK

Because I'm so goddam old, I've made a lot of mistakes. I wrote this book to help you, my fellow Dick Americans, avoid common pitfalls and dangers. I believe that Dicks like us need to help each other out, otherwise we could become extinct altogether. I mean, look at Cro Magnon Man, and the Neanderthals. They walked around, grunting, bashing women in the head with a club, then dragging them back to the cave for some late night fun. These guys were the original Dicks! What's the difference between a Caveman and a Frat Boy? The Caveman has better survival skills.

Sadly, our caveman forefathers were wiped out, probably by some fuckin faggoty group of French queers, with powdered faces, rosy cheeks, and a silk kerchief in their hands. Well, I say it's time we fought back. Dicks are people too, and we have rights. Vote Trump, 2016!

As I sit here and write this book, giving you my sage advice, lessons learned from a long lifetime of taking cuts, cheating, lying, stealing, and not giving a fuck, I wonder if you, the reader, will learn from my mistakes, or laugh at me while you continue to make the same bonehead mistakes I made. I hope I can save you from some grief with my simple advice, and if not, well, thanks for buying my book anyway, asshole!

My second goal in writing this is to make you laugh. So if you don't learn a goddam thing from me, at least I made you smile, while you sit in class, ignoring the History teacher, flicking spitballs at the back of a pretty girl's head, and wondering why she doesn't like you.

A lot of Libtards are gonna get butt-hurt by the things you say. You're gonna piss off everybody. So in this book I'm gonna teach you about the magic of KARMA. If you can follow these simple rules, your nose won't get punched as much, and that's a good thing.

HOW TO BE A DICK

Even a young Dick has seen some crazy shit. Maybe you saw your Dick friend get arrested, because he got too grabby and horny on his last first date. Or maybe you know a guy who tried to kill his parents for the inheritance, a big-time Dick move, only to get caught and sent to prison. I'm gonna give you priceless tips on avoiding similar fates. A Dick cannot survive well in prison, because it's full of even bigger Dicks, and they all get stabby and rape-y and shit. Stay out of there! I'll tell you how.

If you're college-age or younger, you're still thinking with your dick, and probably skimming this book to get to the part about picking up chicks. Your current pickup line of, "You. Me. Sex." isn't closing the deal, it's just getting your face slapped at the clubs. No book about being a Dick would be complete without a section on how to crush puss. I give you the secrets to attract so much fine tail, you can cancel your subscription to AsianAssWhores.com.

After sex, a Dick's biggest interest is money. Notice how I skipped "POWER." That's because you don't need it. Do you really want to be a stupid fuckin Mayor or Governor? Fuck power, just give me lots of money and pun-tang, thank you. With a pile of money, I have all the power I need. In the section on money, I show you how to get the type of job that's just right for you. Dicks are perfect for some jobs, and horrible at most others. If you aren't happy with your job, my guess is you're in the wrong job. I'll show you how to transition, from Burger King Lettuce Bitch, to a job that's perfect for a Dick, like a Cop, a Realtor, or Captain of the USS Enterprise. Money is the central obsession for the Dick, because without it you ain't shit. I will tell you step by step how to become a financially successful Dick. Then you don't have to try so hard when trying to get laid, you can just say, "You. Me, Rich." That'll get her vagina wet.

What is a Winner? That's easy, a winner is the difference between what you are, and what you want to be. I will show you how to magnify your most important skills and abilities, and jettison your problem behaviors, the stuff that is actually impeding your progress, and keeping you from becoming super-rich and happy.

Being a Dick is tough. No one likes a Dick. They are always sniffing around your daughters' lap, exploiting her blonde simplicity. And every time you get fired, or pulled over for speeding, you're usually staring a dick in the face. But we are Dicks for a reason. This world is so goddam dangerous, deadly, and destructive, that the only way our species could have survived, was by forging a leader so strong, so stubborn, and so goddam bad ass, that nothing could stand in his way, not famine, plague, war, NOTHING.

The civilized world owes guys like us a lot. Who do you think built the pyramids? Who built Rome? Who conquered the unwashed savages, and enslaved them, so they could build cool shit like roads and aqueducts? Dicks did it all. A Dick named Pharaoh enslaved the ignorant barbarians all around him, and made them build something wonderful. Yes, the primitives were unhappy, because they couldn't rape each other and pick bugs off their back fur. But the Dick Pharaoh imposed his will upon them, and forced them to make something amazing.

As an Enlightened Dick, you could easily be the guy to enslave some unfortunate group, to make something cool for you. Richard Branson, an enormous 200 pound dick, with a face that looks like an elderly ladies' wrinkled up twat, this guy is a real Dick. He brags about his wealth constantly. He is a very unlikable guy. But what I admire most about this man, is that he had a dream, a burning desire to travel in space. Unlike the rest of us, including all those retarded nerds at NASA, Richard Branson did something about it. He became a billionaire, through hard work and effort, and then he put that money behind his dream, and created Virgin Galactic, the world's first and only Space Tourism Company. Virgin Galactic is Branson's Pyramid building.

Where is your Pyramid? If there is a dream, no matter how big, and it's still stuck inside your head, I want you to remember Sir Dick Branson, and how he pushed every obstacle, every discouragement, and every setback on the launch pad out of his way, so he could reach his lofty goal. Dicks are deaf to everything, except the song of success. Real Dicks are Winners, and winners don't give up until they win. This man, Richard Branson, overcame all obstacles, including his gross scrotum-skin turkey neck, his British accent and awful British jack-o-lantern teeth, and his being born with 6 fingers on each hand, to become the premier spaceman of our time, and also the 7th richest man in the world.

Not bad for a Dick.

Karma

(Or Why Bad Things Happen To Good Dicks)

Karma has fascinated me for so long. It's kinda like horoscopes, in that it sounds like complete bullshit, until you look back at your own life and admit that you see a connection, between how you treat people, and how others treat you.

"Payback's a bitch." " What goes around comes around." " I'm calling the cops." "I want a divorce." "Clean out your desk, you're fired." These are all expressions of bad karma.

Before I ever realized I was a Dick, I recognized the pattern of Karma in my life. To some extent, we have all been trained to believe in Karma since we were booger-eating brats. Be a good boy, or Santa Claus won't bring you any presents. Your Mom might have said, "If you get good grades in school, I'll buy you that nice Huffy bike at Walmart." But for most of us Dicks, Karma usually showed up as something negative, like maybe you drank too much at the nightclub and crashed your car. Or you might have cheated on your wife with some skanky gutter-slut with big tits and bad teeth, and now you're paying alimony and child support.

Karma. For most Dicks, Karma sucks. Payback's a bitch, and this bitch is stalking me! But it doesn't have to be this way. I'm going to show you how to turn this shit around, and make Karma work for you. By following my simple life rules, Karma can be your trusted friend.

Karma is the basic building block for the entire society.

Think of Karma as Social Justice. If you study hard and go to college, Karma says you'll get a better job. If you treat women like shit, calling them bitches and ho's, pimp-slapping them, you will soon be tugging on your black noodle alone. Yes, I'm talking to the niggers. What's wrong with you? Who the fuck told you that women dig guys that smack them around, call them bitches, sneaking around so you can fuck their friends? Do you approve of other dumb niggers treating your mom or your sister like that? Are you retarded? Clean up your act, pull up your pants, stop acting retarded, crack open a book, learn to read. As a race you disgust me. Stupid monkeys need to grow up and act right. It's about time someone told you the truth. Oprah, your parents, they all look the other way when you disrespect women. But I'm a dick, so I can tell you what a piece of shit you are. And because this is a book about how to get laid, I'm telling you right now, clean up your act. Why is it, that every time I see a flashy ass nigger, with $300 sneakers, gold bling around his neck, looking like a cross between Flavor-Flav and a Jerri-curl fag, he's always talking loud as fuck, about how many bitches he fucked? Next time you see an idiot like that, walk up to him and tell me he doesn't smell like old cheese and a pile of dog shit. The suffocating, putrid odor of rotten eggs, mixed with 'fabulous fakes' cologne from the dollar store, is enough to make you puke. A fucking street whore would charge extra to fuck a guy like that. These dirty, infectious ghetto niggers have the worst breath too, they never brush their grille, the smell of rotting teeth and stale beer so powerful it will singe your nostril hairs if you get too close. Their super-funk drapes them like an evil spirit, you can almost see the stink-lines radiating from them, like a cloud of deadly poison gas. (Now don't get me wrong, I'm not a racist. I just hate niggers that smell like a diaper full of Indian food, and smack women around.)

Religion did a big part in shaping our view of Karma. Jesus promises blessings for good people, and fiery destruction for sinners. Jesus is a bullshit myth, like Santa, but that doesn't mean that Karma isn't real.

Let me tell you how Karma works, how to attract good luck to you, and repel every type of bad luck.

Early Man

About 100,000 years ago, your caveman ancestors walked the Earth. Early Man was a social, "pack" animal, which means they were, and still are, very 'tribal'. They hunted together, slept together, and they lived in groups. Over time, they simply figured out that they were better able to defend against predators, and take down bigger prey, as a group. The tribe was born, and if you look at human behavior today, in modern times, you can easily see our tribal roots, the way we don't trust 'outsiders', foreigners, or people who are different from us.

Early Man was very tribal. And every tribe has a Chief. Below the Chief are hunters, warriors, women, children, and the elderly. How do they fit into the flow chart of tribal members? What level of importance and status does an individual have in the tribe?

Every single member of the tribe, from the Chief to the children, are all in an endless internal struggle, between selfishness on one side, and tribal duty on the other. Everyone must put the needs of the tribe first. The tribe has simple rules, necessary and vital rules. Don't rape the wives of other members of the tribe. Don't steal from the tribe, no matter how hungry you are. Earn your keep. Without these rules, the tribe would fall apart.

So how did Early Man get the tribal members to follow the rules of the tribe? Simple. They punished the rule-breakers, and they rewarded the members who followed the rules best. Let's say a guy got caught stealing extra food. The tribe might banish him, or deny him food for a time, or simply kill him. He might get beaten, or forced to work as a slave. Now, imagine a hunter, who is better than all the other hunters. This guy brings home two elks a month, but the other hunters are lucky to kill one elk a month. This guy gets favored treatment in the tribe. He gets more food, a bigger teepee, and a necklace of saber-tooth tiger claws to wear around his neck, so people know how important he is.

Status was born.

Imperfect as this system was, it survived unchanged for many millennia. But there were serious flaws in the early social systems. Too often, a man's powerful selfish urges would win out. For example, imagine a time of famine. It's snowing, and the tribe has just a few scraps of food left. As an individual's hunger gets stronger each day, his loyalty to the tribe gets weaker. Eventually he just says, "Fuck it!" He takes all the food scraps, and runs off in the night.

Because of this, the tribe dies, starving in the cold winter snow.

Early Man found a solution to the problem of tribal loyalty. The Shaman was born. Religion was born. As soon as a child was old enough to speak, he was told that invisible spirits of his ancestors were watching him, always, and would punish him for harming the tribe. Gods were created, and their stories all enforced the rules of the tribe, and approved of punishment of wrongdoers. Rules became commandments, and religion became the social conscience. These myths became superstitions, then customs, then firmly entrenched religions.

In many societies, the Shaman, or religious leader, was every bit as important as the Chief. This is still true today. Who is more powerful, the President or the Pope? What about in Iran, who is more important, the President of Iran, or the Supreme Leader, the Ayatollah? Depends on who you ask.

Ancient Egypt

I want you to imagine a scene in Early Egypt. It is a time of Pharaohs, pyramids, and Mystics. Everyone believes in Magic. They believe in Gods and Evil spirits. They believe in Hell and Heaven. Imagine a world before scientific thought, where EVERYONE believes in the supernatural.

Maybe a foreign traveler comes along, from far off China. He tells the Egyptians about the mythology of his country, stories of other gods, other superstitious customs. But no science.

You go to the Egyptian Temple, to hear the High Priest speak. The High Priest is the only one who can actually read and write. He tells you that Pharaoh IS God. Pharaoh will live forever, and he can read your thoughts! All kneel before the mighty Pharaoh!

Suddenly, in the temple, a poor Egyptian farmer falls down and dies. Because there is no medical science, and everyone is dumber than a rock, the crowd looks to the smartest guy in the room, for an explanation, as to why the farmer died in the temple. They look to the priest to explain his death.

From his impressive gold altar, the priest says, "The farmer has been struck down by the hand of Pharaoh! The farmer was thinking of betraying Pharaoh, and our Mighty King can hear the thoughts of all Men. So he killed this man, and now his soul is being eaten by crocodiles in the Underworld. Do not let this fate catch you! Never think bad about our Mighty Pharaoh, or you will die painful and slow. But to those faithful followers who love our Leader, and follow all his Laws, Pharaoh promises eternal life, with Him, in Heaven, with the Mother of Heaven, ISIS, and the Father of the Sky, the Sun God RA."

Because scientific thoughts like logic or evidence have not been discovered,, everyone has to believe whatever the priest says. The priest uses his power to combine society's laws with mythological stories, so that a violator of the law is now a 'sinner', to be punished by God. If his sin is small he can expect some 'bad luck', but if his sin is great, he can expect eternity in torment.

The tribe must come first. The selfish urges must submit to the tribal laws, or risk the death of the tribe itself.

Rule #1. Trust the Scientific Method

This book is about how to get rich, and how to get laid. I will show you that there are universal formulas to get what you want. The scientific process is all you need.

First, I want you to jettison any religious beliefs. There is no God, and even if there was, he doesn't give a shit about you.

If you were in a nasty auto accident, would you want the ambulance to take you to the hospital, or to a church? God doesn't answer prayers. So stop being a dimwitted sucker. God is for weak-minded people who can't think for themselves, and need a bunch of stories written by goat herders to tell them how they should live.

If you are a Christian, it's not your fault. Your brain is just smaller than mine. You might have that Zika virus that makes your head look all shrunken and caved in at the sides. Trust me, God and religion are just a scam, a silly fairy tale you chose to believe, because it's easier to believe that you are so important, that God literally died for you, than to think that the universe is so big, and time is so vast, that your puny nothing life is as insignificant as a skin flake on the butthole of a maggot.

God is Cock Blocking You

If you think Jesus is going to make you rich, then what the fuck are you reading this book for? I hate religious people, because they are so fucking stupid. If you are fag for Jesus, you have my permission to kill yourself now. Seriously. I'm not joking. Do it. Send me your phone number so I can call you, and bully you into killing yourself, and even smoking your whole family before you shoot yourself.

Evolution is Real

To support evolution, we have the evidence of the fossil record. To support the theory of God, we have no proof at all, just some mumbo jumbo nonsense stories from a time when people shat in a stream, then drank from the stream the next day.

Rule #3. Maximum Effort

Life is all about Maximum Effort. A successful person tries harder than the average guy. He studies harder in school. Works out harder in the gym. Sets loftier goals than most, and struggles obsessively to reach those goals.

Take Hilary Clinton, for example. To become President, she had to first become a lawyer, then First Lady, then a Senator, then Secretary of State. She ran for President in 2008, and lost to Obama. Did she give up on her dreams? Nope. She ran again in 2016, against a dozen other politicians with experience and power, and she bested them all. She exemplifies Maximum Effort.

Life is a futile process, whereby the intelligent Man imposes his brand of Order on whatever he sees, among an eternally vast Universe of random chaos. The moment he pauses, Chaos returns, to claim all his triumphs, and turn them to rubble. A weak Man complains that it's all unfair. He looks for someone to blame. He gives up. A strong Man patiently organizes, rebuilds, repairs, creates, learns, and adapts. I want you to become that strong Man, because that's the Happiest Man, the Wisest Man, and the Richest Man.

Winning in life is synonymous with survival. Prosperity is everything to a Winner, the central core of who we are. If you don't already have this deep, powerful, relentless desire to succeed in life, financially and romantically, you better cultivate and develop this quality.

Winning is about being relentless. Tenacious. In many ways I'm a "hacker." I am constantly trying to get and stay rich, by studying, learning, researching, experimenting. For me, picking the locks to a young girl's panties is a lot like cracking the code to wealth. Never give up. Always trying, and if I fail, I figure out why I failed, and try a different approach tomorrow. But I never give up. Why would I? I can honestly see no better use of my time, than to grab wealth, and collect notches in my bedpost.

Rule #4. Make the Best Decisions

Making great decisions is never easy. And it's normal to stress over the BIG decisions. Should I marry a "Plain Jane" girl who's earned her PhD? Should I buy that house, and move out of my Mom's basement? Should I take financial advice from a book I got on Amazon, written by a guy I'm pretty sure is crazy? YES to all three questions.

Here are some tips that will help you make better decisions:

1. Imagine you are giving advice to a good friend. Too often, we are so caught up in powerful emotions, that our best judgment is clouded. Why is it, that we can see clearly that our friend is in a destructive relationship, but we are blind to the flaws in our own relationships? Pretend you are giving a friend advice, and you will be surprised at how different the advice sounds.

2. Reduce the information to its most basic points. The human mind can't handle an avalanche of data. We are not robots. Most decisions demand that you strip away all the tiny details, and focus on the biggest factors.

It is possible, and even common, for people to get overwhelmed with a mountain of data, worried and stressed out, and forget that most of that data is irrelevant. Simplify.

3. Is your decision reversible? Obviously, marriage is kinda permanent. So are tattoos. But things like accepting a job, moving to a new city, these are reversible, just not easily so. A reversible decision ought not carry the same dread as a permanent one.

4. Open a spreadsheet, and put all the reasons for making and rejecting a proposal on it. Seeing the factors in list form definitely helps us, and prevents us from overlooking something important. You can even give big factors a bigger font. So if you're deciding whether you should marry a girl, things like intelligence and income might be in 20 point font, and her harelip and hunchback might be in 12 point font.

Careers Custom Made For Big Dicks

The character traits of a Dick can be summed up as follows:

- High levels of confidence
- Physically fit
- Neat and clean appearance
- Calculated risk taker
- Sense of humor
- Able to set and reach realistic goals
- Good decision making, good judgment
- Always ready, always prepared
- Good in a crisis situation
- Good money management

CHRIS HARPER-MERCER

- A person of action

- Assertive, being direct about desires

- Willing to learn new things

- Willing to be a bully when necessary

- Can defend oneself

- Can lead others, and persuade people

- Not afraid of confrontations

- High social intelligence

- Strong drive to succeed, ambitious

- You shape your environment to suit you

- Exact opposite of a loser

- Excellent survival skills

HOW TO BE A DICK

Dicks are winners, leaders, visionaries, strategists, risk-takers. What careers are best suited for this personality type?

Well, I personally prefer to run my own business. Being self-employed means I have the coolest boss in the world. I take no shit from anyone. I love being the boss. For me, the very idea of working in a cubicle for some soulless corporation sounds like the worst prison sentence. I don't care if I can make more money as an employee, I simply cannot be happy if I'm working hard to make another man rich. That said, we are all working for someone else. And we all have to follow the rules and laws that govern our industry or profession. Imagine you are a high-powered lawyer, for a big law firm, and you're making mad money. You don't have the freedom I have! I can tell a client to fuck off. If you did that, you'd be fired by your law firm, reprimanded by the Judge, and disciplined by the State Office of Attorney Ethics.

Being self-employed may not be the best choice for you, however. Let's say you are a woman, working as the director of a hospital. You manage hundreds of people, and your decisions can save lives, and your mistakes can result in patient deaths. You are making $200K a year, and you are good at your job. Your peers respect and trust you to be firm but fair.

Should you quit your job and start your own business? Follow your high school dream of becoming a wedding photographer? Only a drooling retard would suggest that.

If you have a good job, a career you love, then keep it, and be happy. Be grateful. But if you feel trapped in your career, like a hamster on a wheel, you might need a change. If you feel tired all the time, depressed at the very thought of going to work, if you can't stand the people you work with, and they hate you too, you should at least think about changing careers.

Go back to the bullet list above, and re-read the qualities of a winner. These qualities make certain jobs ideal for the Alpha personality.

Here are some excellent careers for Alpha personalities. While they differ some in pay and experience requirements, many Alphas have found happiness in these fields, and you should consider them if you are looking for a new career path:

- Realtors
- CEOs
- Car Salesman
- Police Officers

- Lawyers

- Probation Officers

- Fitness Trainers

- Managers

- Life Coaches

- Entrepreneurs

- Stock Brokers

- Prison Guard

Now that I've shown you which jobs you would likely do best in, let me tell you which jobs you should stay away from. Any job that is minimum wage, or low wage, any job that is risky or dangerous, or disgusting, or boring as fuck. Here's a sign that you have the wrong job: Go up to a girl in a nightclub, start chatting her up, then tell her what you do for a living. If you find yourself exaggerating, or straight out lying, to make your job sound better than it is, then you need a change. As a Dick, you have spent your whole life laughing at losers trapped in shitty jobs. If you are in a shitty job, get the fuck out, now.

Famous Dicks We All Know

History books are stuffed and bursting with megalomaniacs and Major Dicks. In fact, you could say that the only full names and titles in any history book, are the names of the Dicks. I mean, can you imagine a history book, that listed the names of every poor ignorant bastard who died in the war? That book would be called "The Book of Who The Fuck Gives A Shit", and it would sell two copies. Everybody else is insignificant, only the Kings, the Generals, the LEADERS, matter. Every ordinary soldier or citizen gets less than a footnote or a partial sentence devoted to them at best. We read history books to learn about the great things that Great Men did. Everyone else was background chatter, nobodies, simple dirt farmers, ignorant, uneducated, dirty, diseased, these losers make up 99% of the population, and are always 100% boring, primitive, and disappointing.

As you read about these Famous Dicks, I want you to look for common traits among them, and ask yourself, "What makes these men so great? Was it their warlike nature? Were they smarter than their peers? I want you to discover the prerequisites to greatness, by learning about the Heroes of History. Then ask yourself if you have the same qualities, and what you can do to improve yourself.

Genghis Khan

In the 13th century, Genghis Khan was an unstoppable force. This man singlehandedly carved a vast empire out of Asia that stretched into

Europe. Many millions died. Khan was as bloodthirsty as he was brilliant military genius.

Like many rulers, Genghis Khan was not his birth name, but more of a title, which means, "Supreme Leader". Real Leaders love to give themselves impressive titles, like Alexander the Great, Emperor Caligula, Pharaoh Akhenaten, and Julius the Caesar. Fuck being called a king. These dudes made other kings kiss their feet. A king was just another dirty savage to a guy like Khan.

One day, in a heated battle, a soldier shot Khan's horse out from under him. Khan captured the soldier, and instead of killing him, he made him an officer in his army.

Khan was famous for getting his enemies to accept surrender and join his army. Most of his fighters were once his enemies.

Genghis Khan was responsible for 40 million deaths. This is amazing, as there were only 360 million people alive at the time. In other words, he killed more people than died in World War II, and he did it without guns, bombs, planes, ships, just an army on horseback, with swords and arrows. Amazing.

Adolf Hitler

If you are a Jew or a nigger, you can skip ahead to the next section. I am not a racist, but I can't

stand the Jews. Here's why I hate those greedy hook-nose trolls:

- Jews are Cowards. Think about it. They were slaves in Egypt, and also in Babylon. I don't have much respect for slaves (that's why I'm not a big fan of the Negro either). To me, a slave is the lowest form of life. Fight back, you fucking cowards. Now let me blow your mind with stone cold facts: 6 million Jews were killed in WW II. Why didn't they fight back? 6 million people, all afraid to fight back, because they are pathetic Jews. ISIS controls Iraq and Syria, and their soldiers number less than 30,000. So why did 6 million Jews walk quietly into the ovens and work camps? Cowards.

- Jews are too fucking greedy. I've been to Wall Street in Jew York City, so I know what the fuck I'm talking about. Just read the fucking Bible, to see how stingy and selfish these maggots are. Jesus described them this way, in John 8:44: "Your Father is the Devil, and the greed of your Father you will do."

- They think they are God's "Chosen Race": What fucking bullshit. Why would God prefer a bunch of physically weak, greedy cowards? If you read the Bible objectively, you could easily get the impression that God hates the Jews, because he keeps throwing one catastrophe after another at them, but like black mold, they can't take a hint.

• Jews are filthy disgusting animals! They chop a baby's dick skin off because it's 'tradition'. They crucified people, killed people by stoning, they bought and sold slaves, in fact if you owed a Jew money and couldn't pay, you became a slave until the debt was paid. These mongrels are inferior, no use to mankind, put them all on a cattle car to the work camps!

OK, maybe I'm a little racist. But it's only because if the human race were dogs, the Jews would be the chihuahua, a pathetic, skinny, epileptic sack of nervous phobias, shaking all the time like a little bitch, with frightened eyes all swollen and about to pop out of its skull. The Jew dog would be whining and barking constantly, it would be retarded as fuck, and impossible to housebreak.

Other than that, I got no problem with the Jews.

And don't get me started on the niggers!

Hitler's trademark tiny mustache has a funny history. In World War I, Hitler was ordered to trim his mustache, so his gas mask would fit snugly on his face. Soldiers laughed at his hack job, and he was so angry, he defiantly cut it short for the rest of his life. This is interesting, because Donald Trump did the same thing with his ridiculous hair. For 40 years people have slammed his awful hairstyle, which is a pathetic yellow comb-over, usually all blown to shit. But just like Hitler, he defiantly keeps his hair the same, essentially telling the world to go fuck themselves. This is the true sign of a Winner. He doesn't give a shit what you think about his fashion sense. He's too busy trying to seize power.

CHRIS HARPER-MERCER

The biggest thing you can learn from Hitler is propaganda. He was a master of passionate speeches. He could motivate the masses, really inspire them with his rhetoric. Study the methods he used to influence and convince the Germans to follow him.

When Hitler became Chancellor, the German people were starving, as a result of crippling reparations. They were living in shacks, while the Jew-owned banks were foreclosing on homes and farms. Hitler bravely kicked the Jews out. For years, he encouraged the Jews to get the fuck out of Germany, but they refused. So he did what he had to do. Next time take a hint.

Hitler created a thriving economy with no unemployment. What other modern nation can claim such an impressive accomplishment?

Hitler was all about family values, and strong women and children. His Nazis were big on preventing animal cruelty, and environmental preservation. Hitler was a vegetarian, did you know that? The Jew-run media is always telling you the negative shit, never the positive.

If you aren't a nigger or a kike, you would have loved Hitler. He treated the German workers well, with vacation time, a 5 day work week, free health care, and trade unions.

Study this magnificent leader. Learn from him. Read his book, 'Mein Kampf', to discover why the Jews deserved everything they got. Fuck those Christ-killers.

Alexander the Great

How do I begin to sing the praises, of a man so great, that his fucking last name is Great? A man with God-like attributes, a historical Superman? Let me try to set the stage for you.

Alexander's father, King Phillip, hired the best philosopher of the time, the legendary Aristotle, to educate the young boy, when he was only 13. This gave the boy-King a huge advantage, as few people could read. His special training and status also gave him an enormous ego.

Here is what started the megalomania for Alexander: His mother, Olympias, told him he was a virgin birth, and that she had been miraculously impregnated by the Great God Zeus. This belief stuck with the boy all his life. He called himself Son of Zeus. Soothsayers and Mystics confirmed this belief, by spreading the rumor that when he was born, the very stars in the sky predicted his greatness.

The triad of success is this:

- Self Confidence-believing you can do fantastic things
- Self Reliance-not needing anyone for anything
- Self Mastery-controlling impulsive behavior, and improving decision making skills

Alexander certainly had the first triangle point, incredible confidence.

Julius Caesar

Here is a man so great, the month of July is named after him. His most famous quote is, "I came, I saw, I conquered."

Quite the lady's man, Julius fucked the famous Cleopatra of Egypt, probably the most beautiful woman of her time.

Now let's take a look at some modern-day success stories, winners we are all familiar with.

Captain Kirk

Don't look at fat sloppy William Shatner! That soggy pile of ham and cheese is no leader. But his fictional character was a real leader. He commanded a starship. He never asked permission from the Federation before starting shit with Klingons or Romulans. He fucked blue women, green women, and he even kissed a black woman on TV, in 1968! Kirk was a real pickup artist.

I also give props to Captain Picard, another excellent leader.

Brock Lesnar

This guy is the ultimate badass.

When I was a kid, half the school wanted to be tough, and half the school wanted to fuck babes. Either you are wrestling guys on a mat, or you're wrestling girls on a bed. I chose the latter, and I have no regrets. I'm not implying that guys who like wrestling, MMA, and football are closet queers…I'm just saying that while I was having a three-way with some drunk bisexual hotties, those guys were all fagging off in a gym locker somewhere. And the fans of these sports are even worse, closet queers, all of them.

But even though Brock Lesnar likes to wrestle naked dudes, and have their scrotum pressing up against his face as they roll around on the floor, he's still an Alpha to me. He is married to Sable, a WWE Diva, basically a blonde Kim Kardashian boner-maker. Not bad.

Brock's favorite opponent in the ring was "The Big Show", a massive slab of beef 7 feet tall, and weighing 440 pounds. Brock is the biggest draw in UFC history, and he was paid a fortune for it.

Like Mike Tyson, Brock has a 'boy's voice', in that it is far too squeaky to be attached to such a giant man.

What's most impressive with Brock is his intense training. Up before dawn, this former farm boy can run down the road with a 180-pound tree log on his back.

Other Notable Dicks

I don't want to bore you with my list of impressive Alphas. I want you to think of the Alphas that you personally admire, and then ask yourself why those guys made your list. Try to reflect those same qualities in your own life. I wish I had Brock's insane dedication to training. Hitler's passion for motivating an angry crowd. Alexander's confidence in his own divinity. The Pharaoh's riches and army of slaves. You get the idea.

I see leadership qualities in Don Draper, Donald Trump, Gordon Ramsey, Muhammad Ali, Mike Tyson, and Clint Eastwood. That doesn't mean I like all these guys. I don't have to like Trump to admit that he's a natural leader.

How To Be A Winner

This chapter is where I put lots of useful advice for you, shit I wish I was told when I was young. Maybe you already know everything, like I did when I was young. If so, please consider this a refresher, a practice rehearsal. And if you think you know everything, then why in fuck's sake do you have my book in your hands? Isn't this book proof that you're an idiot, and you will buy any self-help garbage written by any charlatan or clown, in the slim hope that it might save you from your own fucked up life, and your deplorable decision-making skills?

Don't Stress Out

I know that for some of you, asking you to not stress out is like asking you to not be fat or ugly. But you need to understand what stress is, why it's bad, and how to reduce it.

Thousands of years ago, Early Man lived a very stressful life. He was hunted by lions and wolves, and feuding with enemy tribes.

Basically, whenever Early Man thought of something he feared, he would trigger his adrenaline. This chemical would pump through his heart, allowing him to run faster, fight harder, and feel less pain. All these benefits were temporary! And the adrenaline was bad for the heart.

Today, when Modern Man thinks of things he fears, like getting fired from his job, or losing his house to foreclosure, he stresses out. But it's different now. The stress is much more chronic, even permanent in some people. This is bad, M'Kay?

Fear is the enemy here. Don't be a pussy. Face your fears, and they will turn and flee from you.

Personally, I use marijuana to relax. I don't smoke it, because I care about my lungs. I don't want to walk into a business meeting stinking like weed. I don't want a traffic cop to smell weed smoke on my clothes. So I buy lozenges. Little candies that taste like root beer or pineapple, and two will make me take a deep nap. If I'm stressing out, I simply reach for a marijuana candy, and in a ½ hour I'm feeling very relaxed. Now I'm able to deal with a crisis or a setback, because I've calmed down. My decisions are better, wiser.

NEVER reach for tobacco or alcohol to relieve stress! Are you retarded? Maybe this book is too complex for you? Any dipshit knows that tobacco is for losers, and booze of any kind is pure uncut idiot juice. If you disagree with me, I want you to slap your mom, really hard, for not raising you right.

Remember, stress is a tiny little fear, and fear is never good. Face it, defeat it, and when you turn around to face it, there will be nothing there at all, just a shadow that retreats from your magnificent brilliance.

Healthy Living

This is a HUGE part of being a winner. My personal level of self confidence comes from many sources, but a main pillar is definitely my physical fitness.

Imagine a crisis, an auto accident, a robbery attempt, people trapped in a burning building. Are you healthy enough to drag an unconscious man from a crashed car? What if that man is a big fat sloppy gross walrus? Are you in such impressive physical shape, that robbers think twice about jacking you? Or are you such a pathetic, sissified, geeky scooter -rider, with a beer gut, a bird chest, pasta noodles for arms, that robbers are naturally drawn to you, because you seem like such an easy victim?

If I want to be an Alpha, I need to be in excellent physical shape. This will intimidate smaller, fatter males, and will arouse fertile females.

Now, I'm the first to admit, I'm not built like an MMA fighter. But when I think of all the times in my life, when I seized control of a situation, because the other men in the room were all metro-queers with flabby arms and coiffed hairdos, I am so grateful that I am a weightlifter and bodybuilder.

It must be near impossible, to pick up on chicks, or to push your way through the cutthroat business world, looking like the cast of Big Bang Theory. Bulk up, get in shape, lose your fat disgusting belly.

When you go prowling for pussy, do you hook up with the broad that's 100 pounds overweight? If you do, it's probably because your self esteem is in the toilet. You think you can't do better than a trashy heifer, because you are a fat slob too. Get smart. Lose the weight, and improve your appeal to the ladies. This is a no-brainer.

I prefer lifting heavy weights. I am proud of my abs. When I do stomach crunches in the gym, people gather around, because I am impressive. I'm older now, but I keep my body tuned and fit, ready for anything. Guys rarely start shit with me, because I look like I can defend myself.

If you are into cardio, yoga, gymnastics, running marathons, that's fine. Fitness doesn't mean being a steroid gorilla. But if lesbians are mistaking you for a butched-out dyke, it's time to change your fitness routine. If guys at work are still giving you wedgies, and you're 35, go join a martial arts class, and get your revenge on. Stop being a pussy, you are a dick!

Dress Like a Winner

Remember the saying, "You can't judge a book by it's cover?" What a load of shit. That's the whole purpose for having a cover! A cover gives you a peek as to what's inside.

Your clothes do exactly the same thing. Whether you are in a nightclub trying to bang sluts with short skirts and low self esteem, or you are a corporate exec and want to make a better impression to investors and clients, your clothes tell the world what you're all about.

I like the 'banker's look', it just works for me. I don't try to look flashy, but I try to look like I can afford things, good things. Crisp, white button-down Oxford shirt, no tie. I keep the top button undone, like I just got out of a big conference meeting, and barely have time to grab a drink in a club, before I'm on a plane somewhere, doing big things, making big deals. I AM A BIG DEAL. I know it, and my clothes reflect it. If my clothes aren't new, they are very close to new, and clean. Sharp. My black loafers are Italian style, my pants are dark black, and fit perfectly.

This is called "peacocking". The male peacock displays his enormous band of beautiful feathers, high above his head, and shakes them with confidence. He makes other males feel inferior, and he makes females feel aroused, or at least interested.

A flawless appearance inspires confidence and trust. Impeccable behavior makes for an excellent impression, think James Bond in a casino. What you wear is telling the world who you are. Go stand in front of the mirror, and ask yourself, honestly, what your clothes say about you.

Don't be flashy, garish, or over-the-top, unless you can pull it off. (You probably can't.)

HOW TO BE A DICK

Find a pretty girl, the kind you're attracted to. Ask her what her favorite men's cologne is, then go out and buy that. Don't bathe in it, like an Iranian in a white BMW. Go find that pretty girl again, and ask her how much cologne you should put on. This girl can give you great advice on what clothes to wear, what style of haircut or glasses, mouthwash, everything. Basically, you are a hunter, and she is the rabbit, happy to tell you what it takes to get between her legs.

Tattoos, piercings, and stretching your earlobe until it's resting inside your armpit are all stupid fucking fads, not professional, not sexy. You think you gotta mutilate yourself to look cool? How many holes do you need to poke in your own skin, before you realize how stupid that shit is? Being cool is not doing what 'everyone else' is doing. Be smart. If a doctor or lawyer or CEO wouldn't do it, you shouldn't either. I never heard of a hot girl falling for an old bald guy, because she liked his edgy tattoo, or his pierced lip. But I have heard from hundreds of women, who say that men look gay and desperate with earrings, tattoos, and all that other useless shit. You don't need it.

Don't wear a watch. How stupid are you? Your smartphone is your watch! You are trying to bang millennial hotties, and you're wearing a grandfather's fake-gold watch? The only reason to wear jewelry is to show people you have wealth. Let your clothes say that, not some cheesy rope-chains or giant-ass gold rings. Look professional.

NEVER wear any religious jewelry. Are you trying to fuck some churchy bitches? Why? They are all lousy lays, trust me. Stiff, inhibited, self-conscious, church broads are like masturbating with a partner. You can do better. Much better. Imagine you're at a club, with a big loud crucifix around your neck.

You are reminding drunk girls about church. You should be reminding them about sex, you stupid fucking idiot. Religion is for retards. If you believe in God, go get a gun, and put the barrel in your mouth. But before you do that, kill your whole family. Oh, wait- before you do all that, be sure to go to Amazon.com and give my book a 5 star review. Thanks, shit for brains.

Bad Breath! Brush your grille, use breath mints, see your dentist about the rotten tooth in the back of your mouth. C'mon, guys, this is ABC first grader stuff. When you meet a girl, and you want to kiss her, please make sure your breath doesn't reek like a trash can at a dog park.

Studies show that women are most attracted to men wearing the color blue. Blue gives the man an image of stability, reliability, and faithfulness. Stay away from yellow-green, a color that repels both sexes equally.

If you make a 'grooming gesture', like straightening your hair or tie, it shows you are interested in making a good impression.

Don't fold or cross your arms or legs. An 'open' body position conveys more confidence, and is seen as being more attractive.

Women are biologically attracted to dominant men. Stand tall, shoulders back, with your toes pointed outward. Take up space. Stand in the center of the room. Head held up. Speed up your speech and gestures to appear more assertive.

Now here's a secret about body language. People are most attracted to people who are like themselves. You should 'mirror' the target's behavior. If they talk fast, do the same. If they lean in, you should lean in. Be subtle.

Never cover your face or mouth with your hand. Don't scratch your nose, chin, or ear. These gestures are seen as dishonest.

Facial hair is a matter of personal preference, but for fuck's sake keep your shit trimmed, clean and neat. Studies show that women find bearded men more attractive, but studies also show that a clean-shaven face makes you look younger, and youth always looks better than old. I keep my face shaven, but I use an electric razor, because I believe that dragging a razor blade across your face everyday can make your face look like a horse's saddlebags after a decade or three. Plus, a naked face seems more honest, because it's not 'masked', or hiding behind a wall of hair. It's harder to read the subtle expressions of a bearded face, so people think hairy faces are more dishonest. If you lie a lot, do yourself a favor and shave it all off, so more people believe your bullshit.

Body hair is also a matter of preference. Back in the '70's, women never shaved their pussies. Their cute little twats were all masked behind these vaginal beards. It all seemed very dishonest! Then AIDS came along, and he brought about a dozen friends, all STDs. Suddenly guys began scrutinizing and inspecting a pussy before they just jumped on in. I personally shave all my body hair, because I like the clean way it feels. As a kid, I dreamed of being a world-class bodybuilder. To see my muscles better, I would shave my body. After decades of shaving, I feel sloppy if I let myself get too hairy.

Be careful shaving your nutsack! Use a new razor, and the gel-type of shaving cream. Short strokes, slowly, and don't forget to shave your nasty butthole too. Oh, yeah, and don't forget to clean your filthy disgusting belly button! Imagine you meet some young tramp at a rave, and she wants to blow you, right there at the rave! So you unzip, and she's bobbing away. Remember that while she's sucking you, her nose is right next to your belly button. If your navel stinks, and she gets a whiff of it, she's going to barf all over your dick, and you'd deserve it!

Now, what if you get some slutty college chick back to your place, and you are wondering if she is safe to fuck? You can do this test on her. First, when you are romantically undressing her, do you smell a scent like rotten meat, coming from her vag? If so, you should playfully invite her to take a shower with you. Drag her into the bathroom if you have to. That skank is infected!

Here are some other signs the girl might not be clean enough to fuck:

• The girl has a tattoo on her right thigh, from the Center for Disease Control, listing all the STD's and dates of infection.

• When you probe her snatch with your finger, you pull it out and it is burning.

• When you stick your finger in her, and pull it out, but now you just have a melted stump for a finger.

• When you're finger-bang her, and you can feel something inside of her, so you start rooting around in there, and pull out a few used condoms, and a set of car keys.

• She keeps referring to herself as "Patient Zero"

Wear a condom! This is super-important. A condom is like drinking Diet Coke. At first it tastes like shit, but eventually you get used to it. By the way, if you can taste the condom, you are fucking her wrong. Seriously, I'd be dead right now if I didn't use condoms. And there would be hundreds of paternity cases against me. Be smart, wear the penis cozy.

The Mindset of a Winner

Millions of years ago, the science of evolution gave us species adaptation, which allowed us to change, slowly, over millions and billions of years. If you think evolution is bullshit, then I think your retarded mom got raped by your syphilitic inbred bastard father. Evolution is not a fucking theory, but your intelligence is. Evolution is a fact, and if you get just one message from this book, that message must be that religion and superstition is fucking you blind, ruining your life, and that you can turn your life around, simply by jettisoning the spirit/heaven/God/miracle bullshit, and using science, rational logic, and facts supported by evidence to guide your life and make better choices.

And so, after 4 billion years of evolution, you are the sperm that swam out of your dad's dick, and up your mom's cock sock. Yes, I'm just as disappointed as you are. I mean, it took 4 billion years to make you? No wonder people doubt evolution!

The truth is, you are the greatest piece of engineering in the universe. Some of you instinctively know this. All your life you were called "narcissist" and "megalomaniac". Meanwhile, every other imbecile was desperately trying to find personal confidence like yours, while simultaneously ridiculing your big hat ego. What rich irony.

HOW TO BE A DICK

You are the best at the game of life. You are human. You live in America. You are reading this book, which means you at least suspect you are destined for greater things.

You are a winner.

My job is to make you believe you are a winner. Then make you act like one. Then help you perfect your winning, fine-tune it.

The formula for winning is this:

1. Self Confidence- It all starts here, with the belief, nay, the certainty, that you are great, that you can meet any challenge, and defeat any foe.

2. Self Reliance- To be a winner, you must be able to provide for yourself, independently. You need no

one! Make your own money, lots of it. Independence and self reliance is freedom from oppressive bosses, governments, and even family relationships.

3. Self Mastery- In this final step, we fine-tune our lives. We improve ourselves, by making better and better decisions, and taking action when necessary. We reduce risks, and maximize advantages. We get rid of self-destructive behavior like smoking and drinking, and replace them with life-sustaining activities like working out and reading books. WE EVOLVE.

Qualities of a Winner

• Perseverance is essential to success.

• Self-motivation is another essential.

• Good judgment and decision making are vital.

- Physical fitness and health

- Confidence

- Intelligence

- Able to influence and persuade others

- Fearless

- Good in a crisis

- Ruthless when necessary

Bullies

Bullies are getting a lot of heat in this liberal P.C. climate. The you hear them tell it on the news, bullies are basically rapists-in-training, and are responsible for most teen suicides and school shootings.

If you are a true leader, you are a bully when you need to be. Imagine General MacArthur, about to invade Korea, and some spineless pussy Senator is blocking funding in congress. Would the 5-Star General cancel the invasion, and begin polite diplomatic discussions with the Senator? Or would he grab the little twerp by his neck, lift him off his feet, and punch him in the gut so hard he pukes?

Everyone is a bully! Some people are just better at it than others. In fact, the anti-bully coalition is just a mask for some bully victims, who are getting revenge on their bullies, by using the police, the courts, the lawyers and the media as their weapon. Believe it.

Imagine a couple of lovers, who are arguing about who left the toilet seat up. He's been drinking, and he stupidly grabs her wrist, and leaves a red mark. She calls the cops, and he gets arrested for domestic violence. He sits in jail, where tougher inmates "BULLY" him. Then a judge puts him on probation. Can you see how the woman used the police and courtroom as a weapon? She is the bully!

Imagine you work at RAPECO Industries, and you are part of a committee that's going to decide where to hold your Annual Rapists Convention. Alice, from Accounting, is the sister of the RAPECO founder and CEO, Jonathan Rapesalot. Alice is super-religious, and would lick the cheese off Jesus' ballsack if he let her. She wants to hold the convention in Israel, so she can visit all the famous scenes from the bible, like where Jesus got raped by the Romans. Meanwhile, Ben Dover, a real militant fag, is pushing the committee to choose Fire Island as the destination, so he can cram his back door full of anonymous Cuban chorizo. Ben is staring down everyone, talking over them, and implying that a vote against Fire Island is a vote against the LGBT movement. Finally, you represent a small group of ordinary guys, who want a free trip to the Virgin Islands, so you can do cool shit like ride a stallion bareback across a white sand beach, go snorkeling with stingrays and tiger sharks, and maybe flirt with some young native cuties. How do you get the committee to vote your way?

Be a Bully. And why shouldn't you? Isn't Alice being a big fucking bully, by making everyone go to a war-torn desert, full of unlikable, unwashed, camel-nosed fanatics? And isn't Ben's whole gay act just a way of bullying straight people into backing off? Everything about him screams gay, from his lisp to his limp wrist, to the way his eyes grope you in the elevator. But if you were to say, "I'm flattered, Ben, I know you want to suck my dick, and who can blame you? I'm like candy to the gays. But if you even shook my hand, I'd vomit on you, and then go get myself tested for AIDS. So you see now, why it could never work." If you said that to little twink Ben, he'd skip all the way to Human Resources, and file a complaint.

Alice and Ben are both bullies. If you let them get away with it, you are a pussy. Plan your retaliation. For example, you could remind Alice that the Jews killed her beloved Jesus, and invite her to preach to the unconverted natives in the Virgin Islands. You could also tell Ben that any homo can get laid at a gay resort. But the young native boys of the Virgin Islands are waiting, unmolested, fresh, with virgin tailpipes, waiting and hoping for some nice American fag to bust them like a bronco. Now, if you say these things openly, at the committee meeting, you have a good shot of shaming Alice and Ben to see things your way. If not, try another tactic, another angle. Embrace the real bully inside you!

The main reason that true leaders need to act like bullies sometimes, is because we don't have the time, to explain our reasons, then persuade and convince people, each and every time we need to get something done. This is why parents 'bully' their kids. They say, "Do it, because I said so!" How futile and stressful, to try to explain to a 3 year-old brat, why vegetables are good for you. It's much easier and faster to say, "Eat your fucking vegetables, you stupid little shit, or I'll put a wasabi peanut in your mouth, and make you beg me for water."

Think of a military commander, about to lead his Company into a dangerous battle. Does he ask the troops how they feel about the mission? Does he take a vote, to see how popular this mission is? Does he let the soldiers who don't feel good about the battle sit this one out? Does he hug them, and let them talk about their hopes and fears? No. He says, "Listen up, you fucking maggots. If you don't fight hard, I'll shoot you myself."

A bully is a necessary part of society. A cop is a bully, that's why everyone hates him. But imagine if a cop had to debate with every criminal, and convince him to turn himself in? If the cop had to patiently ask a man to stop stabbing his wife, and please drop the knife? No. A cop is a bully. He says, "Drop the knife!", and if the man refuses, the cop shoots. If the man is black, the cop shoots him a few days before the murder, say at a traffic stop or something. The point is, there is a real social need for a bully.

Nobody likes a bully, but without them there'd be no society.

If you work for a boss, you understand that a boss is a bully. You do 90% of the work, and he makes

90% of the money. You work weekends, and he vacations for months. He tells you what to do, and if you refuse, he fires you. This is economic slavery, and your boss is your master. What's your name, nigger? You better say, "Toby," or you'll wind up on unemployment.

Bullies point out our flaws. They make us feel small and insignificant. What they are really doing, subconsciously, is putting us in our place, which is below them in status. By making us doubt our own self-worth, we feel insecure. We have lost our self-confidence, and we are not likely to challenge the bully, because he seems powerful, because he can see our weaknesses.

For those of you new to planet Earth, let me welcome you. Life is not easy here, and we are all guaranteed suffering, pain, and death. Bullies are everywhere. I know, because everywhere I go, there I am. I am a bully. If you have the misfortune to piss me off, I have so many horrible insults memorized, I will verbally eviscerate you on the spot. I have made grown men cry in public, when I start to psychologically abuse them.

The roots of bullying go way back to Early Man. Back then, we were more animal than man. We were tribal animals, and usually we had to push our weight around, to get anything done. Everybody wants to be King, but behind the scenes there is an ugly underbelly to social power. We have to step on some toes, crack a few eggs, and piss some people off. Sorry, not sorry.

When you bully someone, you are doing them a favor. You are reminding them that life is brutal, winner-take-all. You are making them stronger, keeping them humble, and teaching them about the value of kindness.

What if you bully someone, and they commit suicide? Did you go too far? No. They didn't go far enough. You weren't being too strong…they were being too weak.

You can't be a winner unless you know how to push your weight around. For example, let's say I hire a contractor, to fix up one of my rental properties. I was in a hurry, and didn't check references, and I get a real clown, he's late all the time, he is always over his original estimate, and the quality of his work is shit.

I'd be a fool if I threatened him, or directly pissed him off. That's not smart. That's how you end up with a vandalized property, and believe me, a contractor knows how to ruin a house. What I would do instead, is hire the most thuggish, dangerous negro I can find. A real gangbanger set-tripping fool. I tell the contractor that the black guy is my new property manager. He will be reporting to him now, and getting paid directly from him. Now, when the contractor is running late, the negro says, "That shit ain't cool, honkey. " Get here on time, or you're fired." If the contractor gets lippy, the thug nigger don't play that shit.

Be a bully without being a bully.

When I was lending high-interest home loans, sometimes I had to foreclose on a family, or a sweet, kindly grandmother. Newspapers would write articles blasting me, for throwing a family with children out on the street. And even though I offered to pay their moving expenses, the newspapers demonized me, and made life difficult.

I solved this problem, by creating a 2nd company, run by a friend of mine. The new company specialized in foreclosing. That was all they did. When I first got a late payment, or no payment at all, I sent the borrower a letter, explaining that I sold their loan to XYZ Loan Servicing. Now my friend can come in and legally evict the family, and my name and the name of my company are not involved. The newspaper writes bad stuff about my friend's straw company, and no one cares about that.

See how you can divorce yourself from the ugly parts of being a bully?

Positivity

Kanye West is a pathetic piece of shit. I hate the way he sells the illusion of easy wealth and success, to street niggers who are too lazy and ignorant to see through it. Kanye is married to a half-woman/half-camel/half-silicon mannequin, and an army of black teen losers masturbate to Kim, even though she's from desert terrorist-land, and her father is a cross-dressing circus freak. The entire Kardashian gang is a cancer on America, lowering the bar of decency and integrity to Trump levels of shame.

Wow, I am writing about positive mental attitude, and I dump that load of ranting on you?

Seriously, a positive attitude is essential to your success. If you aren't a positive person, you need to develop this quality.

When I see a nasty car accident, blood and limbs everywhere, children trapped in the car and screaming because they are on fire, I am not afraid of suffering the same fate. I realize it's a possibility, but I am "positive" that my safe driving, a skill I cultivated from decades of practice and experience, will help me avoid idiots on the road. When it snows, I drive slower, and I laugh when I see 20-car pile ups, because this is Darwinian Evolution. What I'm trying to say is, my confidence is not imaginary. It is based on my knowledge, my ability to react physically, and my expert judgment of road conditions.

Don't be like Kanye West. He thinks he's talented, even though he never went to school, and never reads books. He's like Honey-Boo-Boo, in that we are all wondering when he's going to self-destruct. We love to watch some smug rich bastard fall from his perch, and end up in jail or the morgue. How will Kanye fall? Drug overdose? Get shot at a nightclub for talking shit? Go to prison for tax evasion? Will Kim cut off his dick for cheating? I don't know how he will fall, but he's an idiot, and idiots always fall.

Stay positive. If you don't believe in your own ideas, your own talents, no one else ever will. Listen to criticism. Some of it is just haters, but some of it is genuine, and if you listen honestly, you can learn from it, and improve your game.

I highly recommend you read "The Secret," by Rhonda Byrne. This book is full of confidence-building affirmations, and excellent advice on how to turn desires into reality. A man is an extremely habitual animal. We are also extremely suggestive, that's why you called that sex hotline last night, because the sexy girl in lingerie on the infomercial told you to call, and against all common sense you did, to the tune of $20 a minute. It's a good thing you only lasted 2 minutes, right?

When you combine our highly habitual trait with our highly suggestive quality, you have a recipe for enormous success. By repeating positive affirmations throughout the day, you can get your subconscious reptilian brain to believe in your own success, your own superior intellect and abilities.

Everyone needs positive affirmations. We all need to remind ourselves that winning is just around the corner, that we deserve every good thing, that heaven is not some place on a cloud, it's happening right here and now, to you, everyday.

Some of my favorite affirmations are listed below. Write down the ones you like, tape them to your bedroom mirror, and say them out loud each morning, as you look in the mirror. The more you repeat them, and allow yourself to believe them, the greater your life will be. This is self-hypnosis, designed to break the pattern of loser-thinking.

- I am too important to the world, to waste my time feeling sadness, shame, guilt, or regret.

- I make the best choices every time.

- Money comes to me easily and effortlessly. My actions create constant prosperity. I am aligned with the energy of abundance.

- I let go of my anger so I can see clearly. I replace anger with understanding and compassion. I reject negative feelings like anger and hatred.

- I refuse to give up on my goals. I am optimistic, and confident, kind and compassionate.

- I surround myself with people who treat me well. I love my friends and family, and I am loved by them.

- I sleep soundly and easily, embracing the peace and quiet of the night.

- Today will be a fantastic day to remember. My thoughts are my reality, so I will make them the best thoughts ever. My days are filled with hope and joy.

• I am a money-magnet. I attract wealth in abundance. I let go of all worries and doubts. My fears melt away and vanish.

Visualize your success. Reject all negative thoughts. Thoughts become Things. Practice the Law of Attraction, and Positive Mental Attitude, and you will be amazed at the results.

Friends and Success

A big reason you're not successful today, is because your so-called friends hold you back. Every time you get excited about a new business venture, they kill your enthusiasm with negative predictions of failure. When you try to work late to get your business off the ground, they tell you it's "Friday night," and practically pull you towards some nightclub or party.

HOW TO BE A DICK

The absolute worst friend you could have is what I call the "needy" friend. He always has some crisis in his life. Fight with his girlfriend. Police trouble. Can't pay the rent. Car broke down. He's always hitting you up for money, which he swears he'll pay back, but never does. If you added up all the money you lent out, to friends that never paid you back, you could've retired early.

I'm going to let you in on a secret. Successful people jettison friends like that. You have no choice. Either you stop letting them infect your mind with distractions and financial setbacks, or you watch your dreams of success slip out of reach.

If you had better friends, guys who were already successful, they would encourage you when you try something new. They would give you practical advice, and real friends would often step in and help you succeed, by investing in your startup, or putting you in contact with investors and other specialized experts.

Your friends are also hurting your success in dating. When you go to a club, and bring three of your friends, they are indirectly competing with you. Maybe your buddy Fred scores with the hot blonde that you had your eye on. All this "wingman" bullshit you hear about, is just nonsense, an excuse for bringing your friend to the club, so you don't feel so scared by all the pretty women. Bullshit. A hawk doesn't need other hawks to help him feel confident enough to catch a mouse. A woman is judging you by the company you keep, so every flaw of your wingman-friend is a flaw for you too.

Atheism

HOW TO BE A DICK

If you want to succeed in life, you must be an atheist. Logic and rational thought are necessary to succeed in business and in your personal life. If you and I are competing in a marketplace, and we are equally skilled in every other way, but I'm an Atheist and you're a Christian, I will dominate the market, and here's why:

- I will devote more time to my business and education. While you are praying and singing Kumbaya at church, I'll be working on the business' success and expansion.

- I have an advantage because I am more firmly grounded in reality. If you believe that angels, demons and ghosts are floating around you right now, that is a major defect in your reasoning abilities. I predict you will get ripped off more than me, because you expect Jesus to protect you, and he can't protect you because he's just a myth. Also, every time you go to church and put your money in the basket, you're getting screwed.

- You believe that the story of the Universe can fit into a single book, the Bible. This puts you at extreme disadvantage to me, as I base all my beliefs on scientific explanation. If my understanding of science cannot explain something, I accept the unknown verdict, I don't make up some mystical answer just to feel like I know everything.

- To succeed in business, and make really big money, you must have the excellent judgment of a C.E.O. If you are a Christian, your judgment is below average. You have the judgment of a C.E.O., but those initials now stand for Cross Eyed Ogre.

- And if you are a Muslim, WTF? Why haven't you blown yourself up yet? How in the fuck can you compete in the modern business world, kneeling on a rug 5 times a day? Not showering, and smelling like camel urine? And dressing your wife up in a beekeeper costume? You jihadi nutjobs are so backward you should kill yourself now.

- The only acceptable religions are non-practicing Jew, because they don't let any religious stuff interfere with business, and Buddhist, for the same reason. Do yourself a favor, give yourself a really big edge in life, be an atheist. Use science and evidence to help you make decisions, and watch how fast your decisions improve.

Education

Getting rich is more about education than anything else. I don't mean formal degree programs at a University. Those degrees are too expensive, and take too long.

There are so many ways you can educate yourself, for free or almost-free. Torrents. Free internet books. "How To" videos on YouTube. DIY programs on cable TV. Community college courses that cost $30 a semester.

If your major roadblock to wealth is the excuse, "I don't know how," let's get rid of that excuse right now. Here is a partial list of skills you can learn for free, from books and videos online:

- Dog Training

- Welding

- Website Design

- Tattoos & Piercing

- Novelist/Author

- House Painter

- Real Estate

- Computer Programming

- Construction

- Insurance

- Cosmetologist

- Tax Preparer

- Politician

- Kidnapping

Most of today's super-rich are entrepreneurs who got rich by selling their companies or going public. Being an entrepreneur doesn't require a typical university education. A successful entrepreneur needs perseverance, good decision-making skills, and luck. Hedge fund managers and financial traders need educations, mainly math degrees.

If you examine the typical MBA degree, you will learn that about 50% of courses taken are not related to business. Prerequisite courses, electives, and things like Volleyball and African American History have turned a 2 year business degree into a

4 year waste of time, and have doubled the cost of getting a degree.

Here's a partial list of retarded courses, offered by some pretentious and expensive colleges you have heard of:

• Brown University offers a course "On Being Bored." The course "explores films and texts that represent non-productivity or non-desire. Jeesh. Is this one of those phony courses the football team takes, to boost their GPA?

• University of Pennsylvania offers a course called, "Wasting Time On The Internet." Some of you reading this could get your Masters in this subject.

• Cornell University offers a course in "Tree Climbing." No, I'm not making this shit up. Google it. The next time you meet some clod from Cornell, ask him to climb the nearest tree, way up high, so he can look for his Taco Bell job from up there.

- Occidental College offers a course in "Stupidity." With so many self-taught masters of this field, it's refreshing to see professional idiots fighting back.

- Georgia State University offers a course on Kanye West. Leave it to Georgia to smash the limits of the absurd and lower the bar with garbage like this.

As an entrepreneur, you need to study business. I can't tell you what to study specifically, because I don't know what you already know. Take general business courses at the community college. Read self-help books on how to start and run a business. Join forums and Internet groups to discuss business topics.

Economics Majors make the most money after college, followed by Law Degrees, then Mathematics. Fine Arts, English Lit, and Philosophy degrees earn the least. If you are a liberal arts major, you should drop out now and save yourself the time and tuition.

Don't Say or Do Anything Dumb, Ever

That's not too hard, is it? What I'm trying to say here is, most of our problems as humans are not caused by external forces, but by internal flaws of judgment. If you make the mistake of reaching for a cigarette during a moment of stress, you could easily become addicted. Now you are wasting so much time, sucking on that nicotine dick, pumping your money into Big Tobacco's coffers, and getting lung cancer and yellow teeth. You stupid fucking idiot! Are you retarded?

Ditto for drinking too much alcohol, using hard drugs, gambling, cheating on your wife, driving drunk. All these things can ruin your life fast, so don't be a slack-jaw rube, get your shit together, or you'll end up living in a jail cell, getting butt-raped by a giant nigger named Leroy the Rapist.

No Fear

Be bold! Don't be a pussy. You will never get rich or crush puss until you master your response to fear. Worry is a type of fear, and must be eliminated from your life. Confidence, the secret to wealth and getting laid, is the opposite of fear. Figure this stuff out, you broke simpleton, before you find yourself living in a cardboard box under the bridge, and the only sex you get is a sloppy handy tug job from a toothless smelly bag lady.

Here are some tips to controlling your fears:

- Everyone has fears. If you didn't, you would be dead the first time you met up with something dangerous. Fear is our alarm system, nature's way of protecting us from dangerous shit. But when we let our fears consume us, we panic, freeze up, we become neurotic phobic victims. Don't be a little bitch. Man up!

- Fear distorts reality. Fear is an illusion. When I fear a man, he looks bigger in my imagination, deadlier, and stronger than he really is. Fear magnifies the true reality of a situation, and for that reason alone you must reject it. Every time a police sketch artist asks a victim to describe the perpetrator, they always describe him as 3 or 4 inches taller than he really was. And black. The perpetrator is always black.

- Most fear is about a future event. As such, they never materialize. Fear has a bad habit of painting "worst case scenarios" in your mind. This kills your natural confidence. Fears are just scary stories your subconscious tells you. To get rich and get laid, don't believe those stories.

• Dare to take calculated risks. You can't get rich without taking some risks. And when you ask a pretty girl out, you take a risk she might say NO. If she says NO, so fucking what? Isn't there another another bimbo right behind her?

Karma is Real

When I say you should love money, I mean it. If we love something, we are drawn closer to it. And why wouldn't you love a better life for you and your family? Better houses and cars, trips, and a much better lifestyle and better health?

When I see a broke-ass gutter-bum, begging me for money with his outstretched hand, all dirty from playing with his smelly baby dick in some tent city down by the river, I don't give him any money. You know what his problem is? He loves my money, but he never learned to make his own. I can't adopt him, because he's too old and ugly and smells like mildew. Plus I don't give a shit if he lives or dies. Only he can help himself. I'm not going to disrespect my own money, by giving it away to bums and vagabonds.

Consider this: there is $150 Trillion dollars in the world today. And that money is not all sitting in the bank, protected by fat cats too greedy to spend it. That money is in the pockets of billions of people. In fact, EVERYONE has some money. Even broke people have some money. So, your job is to grab some of that money for yourself, without using a gun and mask. This is your only job: Make money, and lots of it. This is your religion now, your whole reason for living. If you weren't Jewish when you started this book, you are now. Personally I think

Jews are mutant bags of poop, but when it comes to money, they have the right attitude. I'm not a penny-pinching Hebrew, but I do worship money, because it worships me back.

Defy The Odds

Defy the very Gods! If God wants you to be poor, tell him, "Fuck You! I'm going to be rich." The beautiful thing about life is, we can improve the odds of getting rich, by changing the way we think and act. Junkies are never rich, so we don't use hard drugs. Gambling, sex addiction, overeating, there are a thousand traps and distractions between you and legendary wealth. Improve your odds by avoiding the obvious mistakes.

You can also greatly improve your odds of getting rich, by starting your own business. By going back to school. By studying business subjects. By getting off your ample ass, and acting like your life matters. Take Action! Go out and build your dream! And when people laugh at you, and you feel like Noah when he was building an Ark, you can find comfort in the thought that one day you WILL be rich, and those retards who laughed at you will be stuck driving Uber just to make the rent. Fuck those clowns. Anyone who slams you for trying to get rich is not your friend.

Luck is self-made. At least a big part of it is. Looking back, I can see that about half of my success came from "luck." But the other half of my success, came from a relentless effort to get rich. A willingness to study and learn new things. A mental evolution of thought, where I reject corrupt and corrosive thinking and replace it with proven wealth strategies. This is the difference between a man, and a great man. The great man thinks great things, and does great things.

Self Mastery

This is the 3rd pillar of success, the last step. We never stop increasing our self-confidence or self-control; constant improvements are made. We learn more, by reading and attending classes and specialized courses. We exercise, and keep our bodies as fit as possible. We improve our likability and persuasion skills. We listen better, and make consistently better decisions as time goes by. We learn from our mistakes, and the mistakes of others.

Associate yourself with positive and focused people. Don't hang out with any bumpkin street trash. People are sponges- we absorb the opinions and attitudes of those around us. Hang with a better class of people, and watch your life change for the better.

It is very hard to learn anything, when you already think you know it all. If you don't know something important, make a plan to study the subject deeply.

Stay positive. Negative thoughts can kill your dreams in the womb.

Self Inventory

Too often, otherwise normal people "self-sabotage" their own lives, for no good reason at all. Think about how many celebrities and famous athletes, musicians, and actors committed suicide. Or drank themselves stupid. Or got deep inside a bag of heroin. Or cheated on their wife, and got caught.

We all do it. Self-sabotage can ruin your life. What to do about it?

You should do an honest self-inventory. A nakedly unashamed assessment of your strengths and weaknesses. Every skill and every flaw should be listed. Now, look at the list of behavior anomalies, or character flaws. Do you eat too much? Are you difficult to get along with? Do you have trouble reading? I want you to accept your flaws, all of them. Own them. But I also want you to make immediate plans to reduce and eliminate all the flaws. Do whatever it takes to jettison bad habits and you will be amazed at how much your life improves. If you know you're drinking too much, don't wait for the heart attack. If you smoke too much, quit before you get cancer. If you are being hindered in life by poor education, don't wait for stuff to change, register for classes next semester, and do your best to improve your potential.

2

How to Make Big Dick Money

Rule #2. Income = I.Q.

In America, 3% of the people are millionaires. So if income = I.Q., and you want to be a millionaire, you need to be smarter than 97% of the people. Here's a secret: want to instantly be smarter than 80% of the population, without going back to school, or doing anything? Just become an atheist, and you're magically smarter than ¾ of the country.

Marry Rich

As a wealth-building strategy, this one is tops. If you are reasonably good-looking, young, and physically attractive, you should at least consider this path. If you are female, I'm sure you thought about this possibility since you watched "Princess Bride". Every little girls' dream is to marry rich. But what about us guys? It doesn't seem "macho" to look for a rich bride.

Play to your strengths. If you are 10-feet tall, take a shortcut to wealth by playing basketball. If you are good looking, at least consider the shortcut of marrying a rich woman.

You need to be an "8" or higher to play this game. If an 8 marries a rich 3, that's a good deal to me.

Is this a scam? Are you going to dump the rich bitch after a year, and walk away with half her money?

That's up to you. I would advise finding a rich woman that you could actually fall in love with, or at least learn to love over time. This doesn't have to be a scam. This could simply be a normal loving relationship, in which she happens to be rich, and you happen to be attractive.

If you never even thought of becoming a gold-digger, what's wrong with you? As an student of Big Money, you should have at least examined this easy and popular shortcut. Heather Mills is the former ex-wife of Paul McCartney. Did you know the bitch has a peg-leg? Google it. Anyways, this skank was a hardcore porno actress, and a personal prostitute to the Bin Laden family, before she married Paul McCartney.

She got $250 million in the divorce. Now she can hire a harem of beefcakes to lick her stump all day. And get this: the bitch is not even pretty. Google her ugly fucking face right now.

All the ugly amputee bitches in the world aren't worth $250 million.

Vanessa Laine met Koby Bryant when she was only 17 years old. She dropped out of high school to marry him. Now she's worth an estimated $100 million. Still think gold digging is undignified?

The most famous male gold digger has to be Kevin Federline. Kevin was already married when he landed a gig as backup dancer for Britney Spears.

Three months later, he was divorced and remarried to Spears! Kevin got custody of their two children, and child support of $20K a month. Personally, I don't think he got enough. Her lawyers were better.

Anna Nicole Smith. Tom Arnold. Every trophy wife you've ever seen. Again, I'm not saying this is a path for everyone, I'm just saying that if you are handsome, and you've tried every other path to wealth and failed, you should consider this.

Crime

Winners are Entrepreneurs. Entrepreneurs are risk takers. Criminals are also risk takers. Should you consider breaking the law, as a shortcut to wealth?

HOW TO BE A DICK

My favorite show is the Sopranos. I love it. I have the entire series, and I've watched it at least six times. Tony Soprano is like a hero to me. He hates the FBI, he bangs sluts constantly, and he whacks anyone who gets in his way. Like a train wreck, he's impossible to ignore. That said, I wouldn't trade my life for Tony's, or anyone else's on that show. My life is much better, and it's because I don't have the FBI watching me. I don't have rival Mafia enemies trying to kill me. Nobody is pissed at me, because I whacked their brother or burned down their restaurant. When I walk down the street, I never worry about police, enemies, or any shit like that.

In the series, Tony has 2 close calls, one where a witness ID's him for a murder, and another where his mother gets busted with stolen airline tickets, and claims he gave them to her. Both times, I felt sorry for Tony. I felt like shouting at the TV, "You stupid fuck! You should retire! Simply promote

Pauli to Godfather, and spend the rest of your life relaxing on the beach."

I never met a career criminal, who retired before it was too late. The lure of easy money is just too strong. Plus, we are all very habituated, and it's hard to break from routines. But I guarantee you, every criminal who gets busted, and gets a life sentence in a concrete box, wishes they'd retired sooner, before it was too late.

Right now, I'm working on a small business. It's a talent agency. I found a sharp lady to run it, because my time is too important. She is a former child star, she knows the business of music and acting. Basically, we advertise at dance studios, and music schools, and we sponsor local talent shows, for kids and adults. We charge our clients big fees, up-front, to find them work in the industry.

We also make a percentage of their earnings. Sweet deal.

I don't know if this business will succeed. I think it will, which is why I invested $50K so far. I could lose all that money. I could also make a lot on this venture.

I can tell you what won't happen. I won't get busted by the Feds for running a talent agency.

I won't get shot by a client who didn't get a starring role in a Hollywood movie. I won't be afraid to walk down the street, because rival talent agencies are trying to kill me.

The #1 problem with criminal pursuits is prison. If you get sent to prison, you cannot invest in any new businesses. Your existing investments will all fall to shit, because you can't manage them from behind bars. And your big, black, muscular cellmate keeps fucking you in the ass, with his enormous dick, it's ripping your anus, but the guards don't care, and you go to the infirmary, and show the nurse your ruined rectum, it looks like an old sewer pipe, covered in hemorrhoid sand scar tissue, and all she does is give you a band-aid.

In my talent agency, or any other business I start, I am prepared to accept the complete and total failure of the venture. When I put up the startup cash, I realize I may lose it all, and that's ok. Each business represents a very small percentage of my total wealth. If any single venture fails, I smile, I try to learn from the experience, and I move forward, looking for even better opportunities.

In a criminal venture, I could lose everything. I could get shot, thrown in prison, my family could be targeted, and all my money can be stolen or seized by the government.

I am not willing to take this type of risk. Not when there are much better investments to be made, with much smaller risks.

I am not you. If you look around your neighborhood, and see lots of extremely successful drug dealers, assassins, and con men, and you want some of that action, go for it. I'm sure I'll read about you in the papers someday, about how you almost got away with it.

El Chapo, the Mexican cartel boss, is worth over $1 billion. But many thousands of people want to kill him. He lives in a maximum security prison, a nightmarish place, awful food, no comforts at all, just waiting for nothing to happen.

Al Capone. The crooks on Wall Street. The crooked politicians. CEO's who cheat. Even Martha Stewart got busted and sent to prison. Think it won't happen to you? Every ignorant crack-rock dealing nigger in the hood thinks he's gonna beat the odds. He thinks he's too slick to get caught, even though he's been caught before. And everyone he knows has done jail time. He thinks he's different because he has "street smarts." Let me tell you right now, there's no such thing as street smarts. That's just what stupid people tell themselves, so they don't feel so stupid. You flunked out of high school, you smoke PCP all day, and the last book you read was, "Everybody Poops", but you still think you're smart? Your brain is a toilet bowl, clogged and overflowing with every bad idea ever. You are so fucking stupid, you need to go back to elementary school, and get to 6th grade, to even qualify as stupid. Because right now you are not even dog-level stupid, you are somewhere between bat shit cray and

microcephalic helmet-boy. The reason you are hearing this for the first time from me is, your momma, that fat ugly bitch who I still think gave me herpes, never told you what a down-syndrome mongoloid you really are. She filled your tiny misshapen head with stuff like, "You can be anything you want to be, chile" and "Anyone who laughs at you is just jealous. Haters gonna hate."
 No one is jealous of you. And you look at no-talent niggers like Kanye West and think, "I can do that!"
 Yes, Kanye is a pathetic retard who made it big, by selling other pant-sagging smelly losers the fool's dream, that someday the world will "discover" you, throw bags of money at you, and some big-ass Iranian cunt will marry you.

The bottom line is this: If you think you are so goddam clever, that you can fool everyone, every time, and that the victims you steal from won't notice their money gone, or won't report it, or the cops won't catch you, or your lawyers will get you off, then good luck to you. I have never seen this plan work for very long. But if you are so much smarter than all the detectives and IRS agents, aren't you also smart enough to make your money legally? Crime is for people too stupid to make their money legitimately. The risk is way too high.

Don't be a stupid fucking idiot. Don't get butt-fucked by some prison nigger, because you thought you were too fucking clever to get caught.

Your Boss is an Idiot

Everyone thinks they're boss is a complete moron. And everyone is right. And yet, day after day, they let this buffoon make financial decisions on their behalf. Your boss decides how much to pay you, when to fire you, whether you get a bonus. If your boss is such a tool, how come you can't quit your job and start your own business? The sad fact is, your boss really is smarter than you, because he took a calculated risk, by starting his own business, and now he's earning much more than you. Instead of being a retard and talking shit about your boss behind his back, your boss should inspire you to start your own business, because if a shit-stain like your boss can succeed in business, so can you.

Marketing and Management

These are two indispensable subjects to an entrepreneur.

No matter what product or service you wish to sell, you must become a Marketing Guru. How will you get prospective customers to notice, and choose, your product? The greatest product in the world still needs great marketing. Conversely, I can think of a thousand shitty products, that are profitable solely because their marketing is ruthlessly effective. You need to learn how to get your product seen by the people who might buy it, in a cost-effective way.

Management is important, even if you plan on having zero employees. When I invest in flipping houses, I don't have any employees working directly for me. I don't have salaried or hourly workers; I am the only employee. But I hire several day laborers. I routinely hire electrical and plumbing contractors. I hire house painters and landscapers. Even though these people don't work "under" me, I still need to know the basics of personnel management. I need to be able to select competent, trustworthy, skilled workers. I need to know what a fair hourly rate is for each trade. I need to make sure they do a good job, the first time, on schedule. My profits are directly tied to my management skill: if I choose a retarded home improvement contractor, and he estimates the remodel will cost $10K and take 30 days, but he's a piece of shit moron and he takes 3 months and costs me $40K, I swear to Zombie Jesus that the idiot contractor would be buried alive in a lonely field, with a pipe wrench shoved up his ass.

Crowdfunding

Crowdfunding is an amazing opportunity for you, because it allows you to ask the public for startup capital directly. Fuck those greedy bankers who stopped funding small business loans. Fuck those scammers that run rip-off charities like United Way and Bitches With Tit Cancer. Now we can ask for money directly from the rube, and no middleman between us and the cash.

OK, pay attention now, because I'm going to tell you how to make $100,000 in just 2 weeks. First, go to an inner-city hospital, in the emergency room. Find the saddest little WHITE girl there, maybe a girl who got shot in the face in a drive-by shooting, and her lips are all missing, her jaw is hanging half-off her face. Then you turn to the mother, and tell her you can start a fundraising page for the poor girl, so help pay with medical bills. Have her sign a release form, and start filming her tragedy. Ask the Mom what happened. Film the tears, the crying, the horrible bandages and stitches on the little girl's face.

Now go post this money-maker on GoFundMe or Kickstarter. The money pours into YOUR bank account, not the girl who got hurt. How much $ you decide to give her is up to you and your conscience. Do the right thing. I suggest 50/50.

There is no limit to how many victim videos you can make and post. Basically, you are Sally Struthers, you are asking the public to help a victim, but you don't tell them how much money you keep for yourself.

Celebrities are cashing in on Crowdfunding, including James Franco, LeVar Burton, and Zach Braff. Kim Davis raised $42K to get the gay troll who lives inside her colon surgically removed. Police officer Darren Wilson raised over $500K for his legal defense, for shooting black kids in Ferguson without a hunting license.

The bottom line is this: Crowdfunding is a magic lamp, but you have to learn how to rub it. Study, research, and learn how to get people to send you money. You may not have to do anything else.

Beliefs Affect Finances

To make legendary money, you MUST have a legendary belief system. I have already told you that religion is a handicap in Big Business. Let me add that ANY unexamined, unconscious beliefs, possibly learned in childhood or passed down by family members, can become a lifetime barrier to Big Wealth.

Think about it: Your parents probably weren't rich, but they did more to carve and form your opinions about money than anyone else. To get rich for real, you need to jettison the bullshit they polluted your mind with.

It's not your parents' fault. They can't teach you something they don't already know. But now that you are an adult, it's your responsibility to inspect your own thought process, and make sure that the decision-making process is based on facts, not garbage.

Here are some dangerous beliefs people carry around inside their heads:

• I don't deserve a lot of money, because there are people with a lot less than me.

• Rich people are greedy.

• It is wrong to have more than you need.

• There will never be enough money.

• Money makes you happy.

• You can have love or money, but you can't have both.

• Poor people do not deserve to have money.

• Don't tell others how much money you have or make.

- Don't ask others how much money they make.

- Money should be saved, not spent.

These "money scripts" are shit-colored glasses that you wear, blinding you to the reality of wealth.

Basically, if you hold any beliefs about money that are contrary to the principles I've outlined in this book, you are infected with the poverty virus. Wave at me, as I pass you on the street corner. Shake your little tin cup at me, and I'll roll down the window of my Bentley Continental, and toss a nickel into your cup. Loser.

Initially, the world simply cannot believe that something entirely new can be done. Remember the Wright Brothers? Everyone told them they would never fly. The brothers began to hope they really could fly. Then they figured out how to fly.

Then the whole world sat there with mud on its face and wondered why this wasn't done centuries ago.

Your path to wealth is the same. Right now, you barely believe great wealth is possible for you. But look around you. Many men have achieved wealth, and many were no smarter or luckier than you. They believed it was possible, then probable, then inevitable. Then they went out and made it happen.

Income = I.Q.

Now I'm going to piss a lot of people off. If you are making average income, you are a person of average intelligence. Period. How could it be otherwise?

The reason so many people get pissed when I say this, is because most people are not successful.

They are stuck in shit jobs and live paycheck to paycheck, yet somehow cling to the belief that they are smarter than most. Wrong! If you work at Taco Bell, you are dumber than the sawdust filler you mix into the taco meat.

Did Sam Walton invent the department store? No. There were plenty of department stores when he started his first WalMart. He made a better store than his competition. Did Sergey Brin and Larry Page invent search engines? No. Yahoo and AltaVista already existed, but they made a better one. And when Ray Kroc started his first McDonald's, there were hundreds of other hamburger chains, but his burgers and his service were simply better. All these men made billions, and they didn't invent a goddamn thing. They took a basic idea and made it a little better, a little easier. Zuckerberg was using MySpace, and imagined a similar product, slightly different and easier to use. Howard Schultz created Starbucks, a slightly better coffee experience. He didn't invent coffee! Now you go out and do the same!

3% of the American population are millionaires. That means you have to be smarter than 97% of the people out there. This sounds daunting, but it's not. First you have to believe that 80% of Americans are stone-cold retards, drooling hunchback primitives with slope-brows and ham-hands. They are not in competition with you! They will never start a business, enroll in a college course, or pontificate the possibility of extraterrestrials. They are Honey-Boo-Boo Duck Dynasty Kardashian Jerry Springer Trash. They are obese diabetics made of sausage grease and dead dreams. They are nothing, and less than nothing. They don't qualify to wipe my ass with their tongue.

College

Some people might claim that college is nothing more than a five-year prenatal employee brainwashing, with graduation as an overrated climax. An indoctrination into corporate droneship, an unfulfilled marriage between you and a life of jobs, bosses, and being overworked and underpaid.

But if you don't know how to do something, where else can you learn how to do it?

In order to succeed in business, you must study it, deeply. Take college courses, in business, marketing, and any course that interests you. Learn as much as you can.

Don't get caught up in the bullshit of getting a fancy degree. Do you want a pretty diploma to hang on your wall, or do you want to focus on getting rich?

Study just the essential subjects, and ignore everything else.

Money = Life

I trip out on how broke people talk shit on money. They say, "Money can't buy you love or happiness." Oh, really? A 6-week cruise around the world does much to make me smile. How about you? Doesn't the thought of a vacation, to any destination you can dream of, make you smile?

Some poverty-people even claim that money is the root of all evil! Not true. Being broke is about the worst thing that can happen to you. You need to think of money as something synonymous with life itself. Without money you can't even buy the food you need to live. If you are ill or injured, and cannot afford a doctor, they will give the liver transplant or expensive life-saving medications to someone who can pay for it. If you can't make your rent or mortgage payment, they will evict you so fast, you will be sitting on the curb with all your garbage bags full of clothes and junk, while other homeless urchins pick through your stuff like the greedy vultures they are.

Money is Life. It is your food source, as you are not a fucking farmer, and incapable of growing enough food on your own to stay alive. It is your doctor too- I have a rich friend, who broke his back in a boating accident. The American doctors said he'd never walk again. But he had money, and after 6 years of super-expensive surgeries in Canada and Europe, he walks just fine now.

Money. Respect it. Learn how to make it. Never be far from it. LOVE IT.

Attitude of Entitlement

Entitlement refers to the growing trend in America, where people think they can have, and deserve to have, whatever they want: and they shouldn't have to earn it or give up anything for it.

Entitlement is complete bullshit. Don't let this poisonous attitude infect your life:

• Relationships: "You don't get my dick hard, after 10 years of marriage, so I'm going to cheat on you, and fuck someone else on the sly."

• Employment: "I'm a college graduate, so I deserve a high-paying job, without starting at the bottom." This is bullshit. If you are a college graduate, and you can't find work at a decent wage, then what the fuck were you studying in college? Homosexual activism? Anal hydrotherapy? If you can't make money after you graduate, after you borrowed $100K in student loans, your degree is worthless, and so are you.

• Consumerism: "I deserve a flat screen TV! Even though I deliver pizza for 10 cents an hour, I can put the TV on my credit card, and pay it off in 30 years. Bad idea. Bad judgment

People with a sense of entitlement walk around with no gratitude or appreciation for what they already have. They are some of the most irresponsible people alive. They always blame others for their bad luck and problems. They seem unable to delay gratification. They are usually lazy and always in debt.

Not only do these people believe they are entitled to certain things, they also believe they are entitled NOT do do certain other things that they find unpleasant. This gives them a shit-poor work ethic, makes them lazy, and even conceited.

What is the antidote for an attitude of entitlement? Developing a strong sense of responsibility. Nurturing an attitude of motivation, independence, and self-reliance. Being able to work hard on a task, and be willing to work your way up to the top, instead of waiting to be carried to the top by a lottery ticket or your dead aunt's living trust.

You are hurting yourself with this sense of entitlement. It robs you of any real success, because it rejects hard work and effort. Be smart. No one is going to just hand you a big bag of money, or promote you to CEO or King. You are way too dumb and ugly for that. Work your way up, by becoming your own boss, making fast-track money, and making better decisions in life.

Inventor

It has never been easier to become an inventor:

• 3D printing now allows you to make your invention prototype affordably, saving you so much time. Don't buy your own 3D printer, they cost too much. Find a company that will use their printer to make your prototype, for a fee.

• Crowdfunding can put money behind your project immediately. People all over the world will see your idea, and if it's not crap, they will invest in it. Study crowdfunding, read books about it.

• College campuses are a great resource for the aspiring inventor. The libraries on campus are ten times better than the city public library, which has become a homeless shelter where bums take baths in the restroom and slam heroin in the stalls. In a college library, you can expect the books to be newer, and better. I suggest you take a course like weight lifting or music appreciation, so you can have student access to things like the library and student learning center. I also love to chat with students on campus. For example, I am planning to make a instructional video soon, and I'm looking for a videographer. I intend to find a student on campus, who is studying video production, and hire him. I will pay less than I would with a professional videographer. I can also stop in and chat with college professors if I need to. I also like to use the college bulletin boards, to find students willing to work for me on temporary projects. I have found that students are generally more responsible than the clowns you find on Craigslist.

• Websites like Fancy.com can help you sell your craziest inventions, right now, for real cash. Go to fancy.com right now, and study the items for sale. Jewelry, clothing, furniture, gadgets, it's all here. Let's say you design and create a pretty bumble-bee necklace, and want to sell it on this site for $30. Simply apply to be a merchant, follow the steps, and poof! Your necklace is available for sale. You can find other sites to sell your stuff on, like the LetGo app, OfferUp, SellSimple, and many others. Best of all, you can save the sales data, and use it to persuade venture capitalists to invest in or buy out your idea.

• Don't worry if your idea already exists! All you have to do is make yours better than the competition. Did Pepsi worry that Coke was already selling a popular product? Did Mark Zuckerberg worry that Facebook was a 90% clone of MySpace? No. All you have to do is find out what sucks about the original idea, and make it better. For example, many people don't like using Craigslist to find a good home contractor, because crooks and crazies masquerade as honest reliable companies. So Angie Hicks, unhappy with Craigslist, created a similar site, called Angie's List. The main difference is, contractors are reviewed by customers. This ratings system makes the service contractors more honest, and now Angie's List brings in over $340 Million each year!

HOW TO BE A DICK

3

How to Get Laid Like Hugh Hefner

Dating

OK, truth time. I am a happily married man. I don't cheat. Here is my story.

When I was banging every slut on earth, I was obsessed with getting laid. Like anything else, the more you practice, the better you get. I had money,

I was an amateur bodybuilder, my confidence was through the roof. I used condoms, so I didn't catch any dick-dribble disease from those skanky tramps, or get them knocked up. I used "burner phones", and fake business cards, so the bimbos couldn't stalk me at my work. Having a separate "fuck pad" sure helped, although I was caught more than once, when a previous skank parked right outside and waited for me to arrive with a new sexual conquest.

Do you remember that Twilight Zone episode, about the guy who dies and goes to heaven…he's a gambler, and in heaven he pulls the slot machine arm, and wins every single time? And by the end he realizes he's not in heaven at all? That's exactly how I felt!

After 20 years of screwing anonymous, faceless broads, it actually became boring. Remember, in order to get them into bed, I had to pretend to give a fuck about their painfully boring stories. I had to remember their names, their backstories, and their favorite restaurants and movies. This is easy when you have just one girlfriend, but near impossible when you have a new one each week.

Middle age crept into my life silently. My hair began to thin, my forehead has some wrinkles. I actually prefer the company of women to men, so every time

I dumped a chick, to be with a new chick, I felt the loss of a friend. The new chick never fucks the way I'd like her to, because I haven't had the time to school her on the things I like. And EVERY chick has baggage. They never let you know up front what kind of psychic abuse they went through, but after you get close, you hear all about it, and it drives me crazy.

About age 40, I began wishing for a permanent relationship. I would tell the tramps I picked up at the club that they could stay the night at my place! I secretly wanted to spoon with them after sex, can you believe that shit? Don't laugh, youngster, it will happen to you too.

All I'm saying is, we all get old. And when you do, your priorities and goals will change. So live it up while you can. Fuck as many ho's as you can, for as long as you can. Store as many fine memories in your head as possible. Because one day, if you're lucky, you'll give up the life of a man-whore, trade it for the sweet life of a happily married man.

Women Are Flawed

When you go out on a first date, you are all nervous about how you look, how you smell, you carefully select the perfect clothes, cologne, and breath mint, to make the best impression possible.

Did you ever stop to think that the girl is just as nervous? She spends way more time than you getting ready. Make-up and hair can take an hour easily. Her clothes, shoes, fingernails, all obsessively toyed with, adjusted, all to impress you.

Relax. This is just a girl. What are you so nervous about? She's smoking hot. Big deal. Either you bang her or you don't. Either way, she'll eventually be replaced by the next flavor of the week. This isn't a job interview. It's more like selling a sofa on Craigslist. You meet, you act nice. You look clean and fuckable. You take her to Motel Sex, exchange some bodily fluids, and promise to call her soon. You save her number in your phone, and put stars by her name. A wild night of sex gets five stars. She's one of the first you call when you're horny. If the bitch is a psycho, she gets an "X" by her name, and when she calls you, just ignore her.

Girls who don't kiss on the first date aren't worth your time. Don't give them a second date. Trust me. Any girl that won't kiss you on the first date is either a cold fish, or she just doesn't like you that much. Either way, cut your losses and move on to the next girl. Frigid bitches are lousy in bed. They are too self-conscious, or stuck on retarded Jesus bullshit, "Premarital sex is adultery."

Now when you dump a chick, be a class act. Don't hurt her feelings if you can avoid it. "Hell hath no fury like a woman scorned." I just made that up. Seriously, if you break up without sparing her feelings, you can get your tires slashed. She might show up at your work and make a big scene. Some girls make false police reports, and claim that you raped her. Lorena Bobbitt chopped her husband's dick off. Scary shit. Women go absolutely cuckoo daffy cray loco if you don't let them down gently.

Here are some tips to breaking up:

• Never tell her you are looking to marry her. Never imply that your relationship is a forever thing. Tell her she's sweet and special, but don't claim she's the perfect match for you. She will use those words against you later. If you don't mislead her by hinting at weddings and "meet-the-parents" bullshit, you can claim that you never deceived her.

- Don't mention any of her flaws. She's already going to be sad, and telling her it's all her fault is going to make her angry. Tell her the TRUTH. You are a slut. You can't keep your zipper up. You sleep around, like a male Lindsay Lohan, and if you were to stay with her, you would only disappoint her, by screwing her friends. Tell her that her Mom looks hot, and she'll gladly leave you and never look back.

- Don't lead her on with false statements. If you aren't honest, and she sees your dating profile on Plenty Of Fish, she knows you lied to her, and you really do want to bang other women. Tell the truth, that you are enjoying the dating life, you aren't ready to settle down with just one woman, maybe someday, but not now. Tell her you don't want to make a commitment that you cannot honor, because you are too weak, and she deserves better.

- Remind her that the time she wastes trying to convert you into a monogamous partner, she can spend with a guy who's ready to love her exclusively.

• You cannot be friends with a girl after you breakup. This has never worked in the history of dating. A girlfriend is incapable of watching you make out with her replacement without feeling ugly and rejected. Plus, how's it gonna look when you try to fuck one of her friends?

• Don't cheat on her. This should be the first rule. If you cheat, she has every reason to cut your dick off. If you want to fuck someone new, you must break up with your current girl. That way you can avoid a botched circumcision by your angry ex.

• Breaking up is like ripping off a band-aid. Do it fast, then offer her a hug if she's crying. Do not argue, no matter how much you want to. Breakups are done best in a public restaurant, so it's harder for her to make a scene.

• Did you know that women have a snow-globe inside of them, and each tiny snowflake is a different emotion? Don't shake the fucking snowglobe! She will seem to be all over the map, angry at first, then sad, shit, she may even laugh. Be ready for all of it. Stay calm, neutral, and stick to the script.

• If you can't breakup nicely, here are a few tricks:

o Tell her you are bisexual. Tell her you want to do a ménage a trois. Tell her you caught herpes, or HIV. Tell her you are facing charges for a sex crime. Tell her you have an incestuous relationship with your mother. Ask her how she feels about making a porno. Ask her for anal. Tell her you're allergic to her cat. Pretend you're gay, then suck a guy's dick in front of her to prove it. Bring out the kink: anal beads, bondage chains, nipple clamps. Tell her you've been hiding a nasty heroin habit.

Plenty Of Fish

I have fucked over a thousand women. I am not exaggerating. Boning broads is actually quite easy for me, because I genuinely prefer the company of women to men. I'm no fag. I don't like gay shit like football, gambling, beer, hunting, and other retarded shit that ordinary men love. Things I like just happen to be the same things most girls like: going to the movies, music concerts, outdoor stuff like nature trails and camping, I love to explore a meadow or field with my dogs, I like to eat at excellent restaurants, and I love to travel.

See how my interests are more in sync with a girl than a guy? A girl on a dating site is basically shopping for a new pair of shoes. I'm a shoe that compliments her tastes and interests. You are a shoe she desperately wants to throw away. You are the shoes they chuck up onto the power lines on the street poles. You are a joke. You actually repel women when you go to a club, because you don't know the ABC basics behind successful dating.

Plenty of Fish (POF) is the largest dating site in the world. If you are on another dating site, you should cancel and switch to POF. Why? Because I have done much research, and the pay sites claim to have better women, but they don't. The very same women on **match.com** are also posting on POF. But POF has more members, and because it's free, more women are using it. Trust me. And don't waste your time on specialty sites like **farmersmingle.com** or **blacksingles.com**. There aren't enough women on those sites. It's a dick fest.

The women on POF are much easier to tag than any other site. Because it's free, and easy to use, it is overflowing with women who lack the money, the maturity, or the education to compete with women on pay sites.   These are exactly the types of women you want: young, dumb, and about to be pumped full of cum.

Here's what you need, to sleep with a different chick each night, or at least each week, on POF:

- Dress sharp

- Smell good

- Be polite and nice

- Treat girls special, talk about her, not you

- Nice car

- Spending cash for things like movies, dinner, concerts

- A place to take a girl, for making out, that's not a creepy basement or your mom's house

- Condoms

- Exit plan

HOW TO BE A DICK

Now before we start, you might be wondering if I screwed a thousand ugly bitches, or a thousand playboy bunnies. Well, I never fuck fuglies, or at least I won't admit to it. You see, I don't drink alcohol, so I don't have drunk goggles. Also, I'm a fucking Greek god, rock hard abs, and muscles that mortals like you can never develop. And my wallet is fat, not fake-fat like yours, but real fat. And when I was prowling for pussy on POF, I drove a black corvette convertible, and I had my own fuck-pad, a condo in a gated community, so no clingy bitches can stalk me and wait in ambush outside my unit.

What you really want to know is, will you be shagging with toothless hillbilly water-buffaloes, or something higher on the food chain? Well, what do you bring to the table? Are you a quality sort of guy? Educated, financially solvent, clean and neat, polite, charming, an empathic listener? Or are you a cross-eyed mutant obese smelly homeless street urchin, with herpes on your mouth and dick? If you have personal value, women will see it. If they look right through you like you're invisible, it's because you need to improve your game. Take a bath. Get a job. Or do what most losers do… lower your standards, and date a sea-cow, it's easier than raising your own personal value, and dropping the hundred pounds of disgusting whale blubber you wear like a fat-suit crushing your overworked heart.

I recommend you open 2 separate accounts on POF. The reason is, there are 2 sections you want to play in, "Dating Nothing Serious", and "Casual". The reason you need 2 accounts is, POF doesn't let you select both categories. So to get maximum tail, you should post a different profile in each section.

Most guys are posting in the "seeking long-term relationship" section. If you really are looking for true love, that's fine, I'm happy for you. If you are deceiving women, by dating multiple chicks while telling them you love them exclusively, this shit will probably blow up in your face. Also, if you are a kinky man-slut and want to get your freak on with chicks who are into some wild shit, AdultFriendFinder.com may be what you're looking for. Wear a condom.

Girls on POF have been preselected for some combination of stupidity, desperation, and sluttiness. Prime hunting ground. In fact, IMO you are wasting your time anywhere else.

Imagine you are at the supermarket, and you see an attractive woman, squeezing bananas in the produce department. Your heart is beating fast, as you gather up the nerve to walk up to her and say, "Hi." She looks you up and down, and a brief shudder rolls across her face as she tells you, within earshot of the whole damn store, "Not Interested!"

You feel like a dried up piece of dog shit. She emasculated you, eviscerated. The shame of rejection is magnified, because you have to keep your cool in the store. You wish you could blast her with insults. Tell her, "Fuck you, nasty cunt, the only reason I said "Hi" is because you looked desperate and easy. I'm a 10, and you're a negative number. You're the reason guys go gay. You are a malignant tramp with lop-sided boobs and flabby upper arms. Your belly looks like you're hula-hooping with a flat tire. Your face should come with a government warning. I'd rather fuck an airport toilet."

Now let's look at my approach. I get on POF, and I filter the profiles, so that I only see girls between 20 and 30, within a 25 mile radius. Then I filter again, by removing all the ugly Shamu broads, the obviously psycho bitches, and the ones with small children. (Children are going to cock-block you every time. It's hard to get busy like a porn star, when some crying snot-factory is crawling around with a diaper full of runny shit. Plus, women with young children want you to buy shit for them, because they are always strapped for cash.) Don't hit on ladies that are very religious, or you will be waiting months to get into her drawers. The exception to this is if she's Catholic. Catholic girls are famous for being kinky sluts.

Ok, so let's say I found about 20 ideal candidates, all young, slutty, reasonably attractive, and childless. I send them all some variation of the same introduction: "Hi, Amy, I saw your profile, and I think we'd get along great together. Would you like to meet for coffee sometime? Or maybe exchange phone numbers?"

Now, let's say 19 women are as rude as that hula-hoop bitch, and send me "not interested" messages. Big Deal! I still got a YES. So I don't even notice the rejection of the others, because I'm busy getting ready for my date.

My ratio is more like 1 in 10. I get rejected 9 times out of 10. But because I cut and paste my opening lines, I can reach 10 women, all single, dating, and local, in less time than it takes you to get humiliated by one sloppy whore in the produce aisle.

Pickup lines don't work. Stick to the bullet points above. Do Not say things like, "Do you recycle? Because I'd like to crush your box and leave it by the curb tomorrow." Seriously, if you aren't polite on POF, and you get flagged, POF won't hold a trial or give you any warning, they will immediately delete your profile. This hurts, because it takes about an hour to start a new profile, and because any girl you contacted previously can't contact you through your deleted account. Also, when a girl sees you again, under a new account name, she knows you're a creep.

I shouldn't have to say this, but have some class. If James Bond or Ricky Ricardo wouldn't say it, you shouldn't either.

Here is an excellent opening line, if you happen to see an attractive lady at the gym. "You look familiar, have we met before?" This conversation starter is perfect. She will say, "I don't think so...", to which you reply, "Where did you go to school?" Now she's talking, you're talking, and that's all an opening line is expected to do.

When you create your profile on POF, think of some smooth title, that shows you are an interesting and sweet guy. Mine was, "Must Love Dogs." A title like this lets the ladies know that I'm a good guy. Additionally, whether you are handsome or have a face like a Sasquatch, you will make the ladies notice you, if you include pictures of you holding puppies. Women eat that shit up. The Elephant Man can get laid with a cute puppy in his deformed lobster-hands.

I highly recommend that you use a professional photographer, to take your profile pictures. The way I did it, I hired a small-time photographer from Craigslist. He met me in my condominium's private fitness center. As I lifted barbells, and pumped up my muscles and veins, he took hundreds of shots from every angle. The lighting was perfect, and I looked like the love-child of Keanu Reeves and The Rock. I wore expensive sneakers and shorts, so the ladies know I'm flush with cash. I wore a muscle-head tank top, one size too small, so I look like I'm about to shred my own shirt like Hulk Hogan. If you are a middle-aged guy, ask the photographer to "minimize" your fine lines and wrinkles. You aren't trying to deceive the girls, but you are trying to put your best face forward. Women use makeup, so you can use the "Healing" brush or the "Wrinkle Remover" filter on your photoshop software.

Tips for making a great profile picture:

• Don't post pictures of you with any other women. They hate that shit. No dick pics, not ever, they don't work, they are vulgar, no-class, 8th grade retarded nonsense.

• Take pictures of yourself at interesting places. The beach. An expensive hotel lobby. A casino. A ritzy swimming pool at a resort. One of you leaning against an expensive muscle car, something powerful and sexy, like the cars in the "Fast and Furious" movies. A super-charged Charger, a badass Barracuda, a convertible Corvette or Camaro. Nice!

• Maybe a nice picture of you sitting in a big banker's chair, in front of a beautiful oak desk, with fancy diplomas on the wall behind you, and expensive gold pens and legal-size contracts on the desk in front of you.

• Always smile. Unless you have a redneck mouth with missing teeth, you should smile. The trick to smiling naturally in a photo? Think of something genuinely funny or amusing. Then the smile is authentic.

• Find the best angle for your style of face. For example, if you are 40-something, and you have loose neck skin, and your neck looks like that testicle sack that a turkey has under its beak, your best camera is from above, where you are looking upward. This angle will tighten the loose neck skin, giving you a temporary face-lift.

• If you are so ugly you make children at the park scream and run the other way, I suggest your photos be softened, by some distance between you and the camera, say about 25 feet away. Close-up shots are not your friend.

It's OK to Lie on Your Profile

But for shit's sake remember your own lies! If you are 5'6", you can say you're 5'9", but don't say 6'.

If you feel bad about lying, just remember that women do it all the time, especially on POF. When a girl describes herself as "athletic type body", when she looks like the defensive tackle for the Cleveland Browns, that's lying. When she writes "average body type", she means FAT. When she writes, "A Few Extra Pounds," she means she is so fat she has to wipe her ass with a toilet brush. "Curvy" means the bitch has her own gravitational orbit.

Dating is War. There are no rules.

You can lie about places you have traveled to, but remember everything you claim is true on your profile.

Drop hints during the first date that your parents are rich. Be vague about your income and wealth, but keep hinting that you own several lucrative businesses. When she presses you for details, turn the conversation back to her favorite subject, herself.

The Hooker With The Heart of Gold

This is a very effective persona. Pretend you are a dashing Playboy, like Charlie Sheen on 2 ½ Men. But you are becoming bored with the dating scene, and want to settle down. Your hope is that maybe the girl sitting in front of you might be the one to inspire you to give up the game. Don't actually say these things to her, but let her make those conclusions about you.

Dating is a numbers game. Rejection loses its sting fast, because there are literally millions of single girls online trying to get laid. Don't try to convert girls who aren't sure if they like you. Just smile and move on to the next girl.

POF no longer lets you "cut and paste" the same response to multiple women. To get around this, you should open each girls' profile in a new tab. Then look for something unique about each girl to compliment her on. "LMAO about your wild Spring Break. Seriously though, you seem interesting and I'd like to get to know you better, my name is X." Then do the same to all the other girls' tabs.

After you message her back and forth a total of 3 times, hit her with, "I'd like to get to know you better, why don't you give me your number and I'll text you."

Don't waste time with non-responders. Don't get your feelings hurt. There are simply too many easy women to bang on this site, why are you whining about the ones that got away?

Here are some average stats on POF, to give you an idea of what your success rate should be:

- 20% of the women you contact should reply back to you

- 10% should give you their phone number

- 5% should give you a first date

- 2% should give you sex

Conclusion: to have sex with one woman, you need to send out 50 opening messages.

Tinder

If you want an app that is specifically designed for Internet Whoring, you should check out Tinder.

Cialis

If you need help getting and keeping a chubby, get some Viagra. Don't put all the effort and expense, into meeting a girl half your age for a dinner date, only to disappoint her later in the bedroom. Fuck her brains out, Grampa, and make a memory that will last you a lifetime.

CHRIS HARPER-MERCER

Made in the USA
Las Vegas, NV
25 January 2025